JOHN PENTON
AND THE OFF-ROAD
MOTORCYCLE REVOLUTION

JOHN PENTON
AND THE OFF-ROAD
MOTORCYCLE REVOLUTION

by Ed Youngblood

A Whirlaway Book
Whitehorse Press
North Conway, New Hampshire

Cover photo by Jerry West
Cover design by J. Christian Youngblood

We recognize that some words, model names and designations mentioned herein are the property of the trademark holder. We use them for identification purposes only.

The names Whirlaway and Whitehorse Press are trademarks of Kennedy Associates.

Whitehorse Press books are also available at discounts in bulk quantity for sales and promotional use. For details about special sales or for a catalog of motorcycling books and videos, write to the publisher:

Whitehorse Press
P.O. Box 60
North Conway, New Hampshire 03860–0060
Phone: 603-356-6556 or 800-531-1133
E-mail: Orders@WhitehorsePress.com
Internet: www.WhitehorsePress.com

ISBN 1-884313-21-3

5 4 3 2

Printed in the United States

Success does not come from setting records, accumulating wealth, establishing a business, or erecting monuments. People are the name of the game. To have success you must build upon the immortal mind with love: without prejudice or greed.

John Alfred Penton
October 15, 1988

Contents

Foreword

My first contact with John Penton was explosive.

I was kneeling alongside the trail during the 1962 Sandy Lane National Enduro, replacing yet another Woodruff key on my Triumph's countershaft sprocket. Suddenly, the handlebar of Penton's motorcycle rapped the back of my helmet at what was probably 24 mph. It gave me double vision in one eye and triple vision in the other until my heart started to beat again.

A spectator who'd heard the impact told me that it was a BMW single running BSA forks that had almost decapitated me (Ed Youngblood's finely researched story informs us that Penton actually used Ariel forks on that Beemer). There was *one,* just one, BMW entered that day—it was under John Penton, and he won the thing.

I felt no animosity over the incident; indeed, if I could have won the 'Lane by rapping 47 guys on the helmet I would have been overjoyed to do it.

Brother Bill was actually the first Penton, in 1953, to win the Sandy Lane National. John's first overall win was in 1960 with his NSU, a motorcycle that, as Youngblood notes, had much in common with sewing machines. Their cam shaft drive, I believe, was designed on Mars by intelligent grasshoppers.

John Penton went on to take the treasured Sandy Lane Wagon Wheel Trophy once again in 1964—with the very same BMW that almost took my head off, and I wouldn't be surprised if the handlebars had a bit more "bend" on the right side than on the left.

I remember that over fifty percent of the motorcycles at that '62 National enduro were Triumphs, which perennial National Champ Bill Baird rode. A salting of BSAs and Matchless machines, and even a few diehard Harley K-models filled out the field. Later, primarily because of Dick Burleson's remarkable performance, hard-core riders switched to Husqvarna machines, until the brand shot themselves in the foot with poor customer service.

The top riders in my enduro club, New Jersey's Meteor M.C., were all riding Pentons at one time. As this is written, they, their sons, and grandsons, are riding KTMs, direct descendants of John Penton's vision of combining the best of the best, admitting and correcting glitches, and treating owners with sincere respect.

Ed Hertfelder
Tucson, Arizona
1999

Introduction and Acknowledgments

In 1968 I took a position as editor of *Cycle News East,* my first job in the motorcycle industry. The Penton motorcycle had just been introduced, and Chuck Clayton, my publisher, asked me to get an interview with John Penton. I went to Penton Imports, expecting to find a man in a necktie who would sit ceremoniously behind a large desk while I interviewed him. What I found instead was a man in green work clothes who expected me to interview him while he roared around a warehouse on a forklift, moving crates of motorcycles. This was John Penton. He was not trying to be uncooperative. He just couldn't understand why someone should quit working to answer some questions. I thought sure I was going to get fired, and, in fact, nothing from that encounter ever made it into print.

In March of 1999, just after I retired from 28 years of service with the American Motorcyclist Association, I had dinner with Davey Coombs, publisher of *Racer X Illustrated.* Davey said he would like to publish a feature on the life and influence of John Penton. I said, "Heck, I can give you that. I've known John for 30 years, and I last saw him just two months ago."

This time John granted me a conventional interview, and we talked quietly at his home in Amherst for most of an afternoon. *Racer X Illustrated* got its story, but in the process of writing it I realized how impossible and inappropriate it was to reduce John Penton to a magazine article format. Besides, my afternoon chatting with John brought home to me what remarkable changes we had both witnessed in motorcycling over the three decades we had known each other. I knew that a book was called for, and I realized how seldom we take the opportunity to chronicle a major period in our history while the principals are still alive to talk about it.

Shortly thereafter, I learned that the Penton Owners Group (POG) had been talking about the need for a book about John Penton and the marque. POG president Al Buehner kindly placed me on the agenda for their next meeting, and out of that exciting and animated discussion came a cooperative plan: I would undertake the project, to which the POG would apply its considerable resources, consisting of personal knowledge, archives, contacts, and valuable advice.

Completing this project has been one of the most enjoyable and gratifying experiences in my life. It seemed that almost everyone I contacted became filled with enthusiasm to see a book

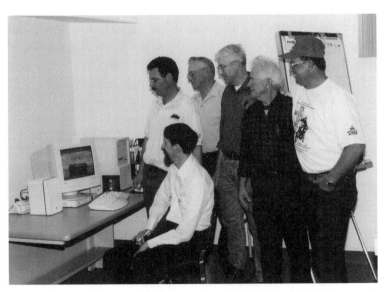

Board members of the Penton Owners Group review the club's Internet web site (www.PentonUSA.org). Seated: President Al Buehner. Standing from left to right: Jack Penton, Doug Wilford, Al Borer, Al Born, and Paul Danik.

about John Penton, and many went far beyond the call of duty to assist me with research and information. There are so many I need to thank.

First, I must thank John Penton for his patience and his sincere effort to answer my questions during six separate interviews amounting to more than 14 hours of interrogation. And that doesn't even count the 16-hour road trip to Ft. Smith, Arkansas, when he and Dane Leimbach took me to the Leroy Winters Six Days' Reunion, an absolutely priceless experience.

I want to thank the Penton Owners Group for its support and encouragement, and for giving me access to its enthusiastic members throughout America.

I also must thank the American Motorcyclist Association, whose staff I pestered for historical information and whose bound copies of *American Motorcyclist* I dug through for many, many hours. Likewise, I should thank the American Motorcycle Heritage Foundation, which has the only full collection of *Cycle News* this side of the home office in California.

For invaluable archival support, I must also thank the Federation Internationale de Motocycliste. Its press relations staff generously donated many hours to searching historical records to which I would not have had access unless I'd bought an expensive airplane ticket to Geneva, Switzerland.

For their contributions to my research I also would like to thank Bill Bagnall, Bill Baird, Bob Bennett, Michael Bondy, John and Jeff Borer, Al Born, Don Brown, Al Buehner, Dick Burleson, Rod Bush, Ron Carbaugh, Tom Clark, Sharon Clayton, Carl Cranke, Kalman Cseh, Paul Danik, Paul Dean, David Duarte, Bud Ekins, Don Emde, Kristin Fitzpatrick, Ed Hertfelder, Bob Hicks, Millie Horky, J.R. Horne, Mary Penton Kovach, Ted Lapadakis, Lars Larsson, Jack Lehto, Dane Leimbach, Patricia Penton Leimbach, Mike Lewis, Larry Maiers, Guy Maitre, Roy Mauldin, Tom McDermott, Norm Miller, Jack Moss, Dave Mungenast, Joe Parkhurst, Donna Penton, Ike and Alice Penton, Jack Penton, Jeff Penton, Tom Penton, Marc Petrier, Dave Rathbun, Boyd Reynolds, Kenny Roberts, Richard Sanders, Malcolm Smith, Kathie Towne,

Barb and Matt Weisman, Jerry West, Doug Wilford, and Bart, Michael, Patti, Paula, and Robin Winters.

I appreciate the faith of Whitehorse Press, who agreed to publish this book on the strength of a relatively vague outline. Thanks go to Jerry West for providing the cover photo, taken at the International Six Days' Trial at Garmisch-Partenkirchen in 1969, and to my son Chris for designing this book's cover. Thanks also to my son Ruben for providing reality checks over the manuscript, and especially to Pat Leimbach for allowing me to reprint some of her wonderful writings.

And finally, I must thank my wife Margaret for not once saying during the term of this project, "Okay, now it's time to get a real job." She knew how much it meant to me and respected those feelings, whether or not they were wise or well-advised.

If I'd been given three wishes before completing the project, they would have been that Erik Trunkenpolz, Leroy Winters, and Ted Penton had lived to be interviewed for this book.

I will consider this project successful if those who read this book experience just a fraction of the pleasure I have experienced in writing it.

Ed Youngblood

1

Milieu for Revolution

It was not the automobile that first gave mankind the freedom of rapid personal mobility throughout the industrialized world, it was the motorcycle. During the early days of this century, literally thousands of inventors throughout North America and Europe were finding ways to hook up small internal combustion engines to bicycle-like vehicles. Between 1900 and 1920, there were more than 500 motorcycle brands introduced in Europe and as many as 200 in America. In an era when automobiles were still limited-production toys for the wealthy, motorcycles were affordable and available to the public in large numbers. They were exciting things, drawing huge crowds to watch the factory teams race on large, oval race tracks throughout America. Daily newspapers regularly reported on the motorcycle sport and published the race results. In addition to Indian and Harley-Davidson, there were Merkel, Ace, Henderson, Excelsior, Wagner, Dayton, Pierce, Royal Pioneer, Pope, Thor, Metz, Reading Standard, Cleveland, Emblem, Yale, and many, many other manufacturers. For motorcycling, these were the Glory Days.

All this abruptly changed with the social upheaval and worldwide economic depression that followed World War I. First, Henry Ford—who, incidentally, was a friend and associate of John Penton's grandfather—figured out how to produce an automobile as cheaply as a motorcycle. Then, the crash on Wall Street in 1929 wiped out most of the companies that had not already fallen under the narrow tires of the ubiquitous Tin

Lizzy. By 1930, America's vast young motorcycle industry had declined to only three factories: Excelsior, Indian, and Harley-Davidson. Then, in 1931, Ignaz Schwinn, owner of the Excelsior brand, decided there was no future in motorcycles and turned his attention strictly to bicycles, leaving only Harley and Indian to battle over a dwindling market share while they looked toward an uncertain future.

These were bad times for motorcycling. The remaining two once-grand companies that had sold their products worldwide turned inward and focused strictly on surviving in the domestic marketplace, some way, somehow. The American Motorcyclist Association was created to play a vital role in that effort: to find ways for people to enjoy and wear out their motorcycles, so maybe they would someday—hopefully—buy a new one. But nothing really changed until the economic expansion that arrived following World War II, and by that time even Indian was well on its way to oblivion.

The post-war Marshall Plan, which stimulated international trade, brought a flood of new, exciting, and inexpensive motorcycle products into the American market. The 1950s saw a British and European invasion, followed a decade later by the Japanese. From Europe came BSA, Triumph, Norton, Royal Enfield, Ariel, Matchless, Maico, AJS, BMW, NSU, DKW, Adler, Horex, Zundapp, Husqvarna, Puch, CZ, Jawa, Simson, Bultaco, Ossa, Montesa, Ducati, Parilla, Moto Guzzi, and many more. Japan introduced Yamaha, Honda, Suzuki, Kawasaki, Bridgestone, Yamaguchi, Hodaka, and others. During this era more than 50 brands were available in America. It was not exactly the Glory Days, but it was certainly motorcycling's second Golden Age.

The post-war economic growth also brought sweeping social change. A new generation of Americans was breaking loose and trying new ideas. The Salk vaccine and other biochemical breakthroughs helped people overcome their fear of communicable disease, allowing people to travel and mix with communities they previously would have avoided. The Pill changed sexual behavior, reducing gender-based limitations and altering the structure and role of the family. Television and subsequent electronic media developments brought the world into our living rooms, for better or worse. Music—the leading cultural medium of the era—became electronic and international. Scientific discoveries seemed to conflict with centuries-old religious beliefs. Neil Armstrong stood on the moon, and a photograph of our small, blue planet taken from outer space made us truly understand that Earth's resources are finite. Timothy Leary used LSD to launch us into inner space. Martin Luther King pointed out that America really was an apartheid nation, and that we should do something about it. Symbolically, the zenith took place in 1969 at a muddy field near Woodstock, New York, where the largest generation in America's history sang songs declaring that they no longer trusted their parents, the government, and the idea of war as the sole solution to conflict. To paraphrase Bob Dylan in one of the great anthems of the era, "The times, they were a'changin'."

Within this macrocosmic milieu of revolution, similar and parallel changes were taking place in the microcosm of American motorcycling. The old rules no longer applied. The status quo was being rejected. New ideas were being tested. And a rapidly expanding population of young motorcycle owners was challenging the concept that a central governmental authority—like the AMA—could always be trusted to deliver the right solutions.

Throughout the 50s, motorcyclists in America were still a homogenous community. Basically, one kind of product was available, and it was designed to provide comfort on the road. People who wanted to race and ride off the road just stripped the fenders and lighting off their big, cushy Harleys, or their relatively big, cushy British bikes, and did the best they could.

But people's ideas about how to enjoy their motorcycles began to change. Just removing the lights and fenders from big road bikes was no longer satisfying. Post-war metallurgy and a breakthrough in the efficiency of the two-stroke engine resulted in a purpose-built off-road motorcycle. Motorcycle design became segmented and specialized. Communication changed as motorcycle publications began to sharpen their focus, turning away from broad interests to chase after emerging, specialized markets. American motorcyclists began to take an interest in international motorcycle sports. *On Any Sunday* hit the movie theaters in 1971 and taught us that motorcycling is a family activity. Marlon Brando's Johnny showed us that being a motorcyclist wasn't so neat; Michael Parks' Bronson showed us that it was. So motorcycling ended up enormously confused in the eyes of the public, and it remains so today, admired and despised, but rarely ignored. That confusion may have been well illustrated in *Easy Rider,* which struggled to romanticize drug dealers and dropouts.

The emergence of the purpose-built, off-road motorcycle gave millions of Americans a new freedom to travel to places they had never been before. But it also drove environmentalists wild, and conflicting ideas about the use of land and public resources by an expanding and more mobile population resulted in government intervention. Anticipating and coping with the actions of state and federal regulators became a new and unwelcome aspect in the design and use of motorcycles. For these reasons, the American Motorcyclist Association had to reinvent itself and expand its mission into aggressive government relations, and to some it seemed like having fun on a motorcycle had begun to feel a lot like hard work.

With the 1970s came the so-called energy crisis, as well as radical fluctuations in international currency markets. Product specialization and government regulation had made motorcycles more expensive to produce. The falling dollar only added to the price Americans paid for foreign-built motorcycles. A relatively brief period of hysteria fomented by a do-gooder administration within the National Highway Traffic Safety Administration attempted to condemn motorcycling as a whole. And both Richard Nixon and Jimmy Carter issued executive orders that limited the use of motorized vehicles on public lands. By the mid-70s, the motorcycle market had begun a precipitous downward trend that would not abate for the next 15 years. The Motorcycle Industry Council tried to put on its best face by talking about how motorcycling had become "a mature industry."

Looking backward, it is evident that the quarter century from 1950 to 1975 was one of the most revolutionary, productive, and exciting periods that American motorcycling has ever known. It was driven by a crazy quilt of chaotic scientific, industrial, economic, and social influences that historians and sociologists are still trying to understand and explain. Although this revolution affected motorcycling in many ways, one of the most obvious changes was embodied in the design, evolution, and expanding popularity of the lightweight, off-road motorcycle.

It would be foolish to give any one nation, company, or person credit for the off-road motorcycle revolution. However, there is no doubt that one of the most influential players was John Penton. Whether it involved changing the product, internationalizing the industry, exploring new kinds of communication, introducing new forms of motorcycle sport, or revolutionizing the AMA, John Penton seems to have had his hand in it. John Penton, his family, and an extended family of loyal employees, friends, and customers helped forever change motorcycling in America and throughout much of the world.

2

The Pentons of Amherst

The Pentons are a family of at least 450 American households that can be traced back to Hampshire, Great Britain, as early as 1167. The line from which John Penton descended had emigrated first to Canada, then to the United States. John Penton's grandfather Henry was born in Owen Sound, Ontario, in 1863, and he became a student of the emerging technologies of electricity and steam. He worked in shipping on Lake Huron and became a maritime engineer. Relocating the family to Detroit, Penton became a friend and neighbor of Henry Ford. Penton helped Ford cast flywheels and machine heavier parts that he could not produce on the little lathe in his shop, and Ford encouraged him to become a partner in his automotive venture. Though they remained friends, Penton would not consider it. He loved the clean, smooth power of steam, and despised the noisy, stinking, messiness of the internal combustion engine—the device through which his grandsons would one day make their mark. Eventually he started his own consulting business as a naval architect, located in Cleveland. Henry's brother, John Augustus, founded Penton Publishing, a huge concern later renamed Penton Media.

Henry's son Harold was expected, like the other men in his family, to pursue engineering or some line of education that would be acceptable in Cleveland society where his family was prominent. Instead, after a stint working for uncle Jack at Penton Publishing, Harold pursued an education in horticulture, and on June 18, 1917, he married Nina Musselman, a

The Amherst Pentons, circa 1931. Left to right are Ike, Ted, John, father Harold, Bill, Henry, Mary, mother Nina, and Pat (Penton family photo).

country girl of German descent from the small town of Cecil, Paulding County, in western Ohio. Harold and Nina had met at Ohio State University.

Harold's choices of wife and profession were not appreciated by his father, who signaled his son's exile from the family by purchasing and giving him 80 acres of land in Amherst, a small community near Lake Erie midway between Cleveland and Sandusky, Ohio. Except for the gift of the Amherst land, Harold was otherwise cut off from the Penton family resources. Thus began the Amherst Pentons, who would later become an influential family in their own right.

Harold and Nina settled on the farm in 1917 and set about cultivating their land, building a productive truck farm and fruit orchard. They offered produce on a stand along North Ridge Road and delivered the rest to market in Cleveland. Like typical farming couples of the era, they also produced a large family. Eric, called Ike, was born on May 14, 1918. Next came

Ted, born June 22, 1919; then Hank, born June 17, 1921; then Mary on December 3, 1922. A fourth son, John, was born on August 19, 1925; followed by Patricia on October 25, 1927; and Bill on April 3, 1929. An eighth child died in infancy.

During his student years at Ohio State University, Harold had purchased a 1914 Harley-Davidson to provide basic transportation between his home in Cleveland and the OSU campus in Columbus. This motorcycle would prove a fateful influence in the development of the Amherst Pentons. Ted once wrote in *Motorcyclist*, "As youngsters we climbed over this gem and pretended to be great hill climbers and racers. In our magic world of make-believe we must have ridden hundreds of thousands of miles while we dreamed of the years to come." John recalls he and his siblings standing along North Ridge Road, watching bikes come by on trailers on the way to a local hill climb, hoping that one of the tow vehicles would break down and stop so they could get a closer look at the motorcycle.

At the age of fourteen, Ike dragged the long-neglected Harley out of the barn and got it running. Although it was well known among the Penton kids that their mom didn't much like the motorcycle, Ike's restoration project was carried out with the unofficial approval of his father, who helped him locate some parts. Soon Ike was riding the first of countless motorcycles that would be owned by the Penton boys. Finding it somewhat worse for wear one morning, Ike finally extracted from Ted an admission that he had sneaked it out and bounced it off a car during the night. Ted would always be known as the wild one in the family. Other members of the family have found gentler ways of saying it: "Ted was the rowdy one," or, "Ted was always rambunctious." Perhaps Patricia states it most tactfully when she explains, "Ike and Hank were a better influence on us younger kids than Ted was."

But Ted eventually would become the strongest ally of his younger brother John's relentless pursuit of a better motorcycle. Ted's inherent ingenuity for solving technical problems, supported by his and Ike's skills as machinists, would give John the wherewithal he needed to explore and perfect his personal vision of the ideal off-road motorcycle. While the

Amherst Pentons would never go far from the land and the agrarian legacy handed down by their father, motorcycles would feature prominently in their lives.

John's older sister, Mary Kovach, says, "Ike used to take me on the back of the Harley to hill climbs. It seems like there was one almost every weekend in those days." Later, Ike purchased a 1933 Harley and took his bride Alice on it for their honeymoon. Alice says, "We had 25 dollars. We went until we had spent exactly half our money, then we turned around and started back to Amherst." Mary adds, "It seems like the boys spent all of their time with motorcycles. I looked up to them because it was kind of a daredevil thing, and they brought home some pretty exciting characters that mother didn't approve of." Indeed, the Penton name would eventually become synonymous with off-road motorcycling, proudly emblazoned on the gas tanks of some of the world's most popular competition machines. John claims that many years later his mother would remark, "None of this would have happened if we had just got rid of that old Harley!"

To understand the development of the Amherst Pentons, Patricia Penton Leimbach explains that it must be viewed as a family in two segments, divided by the untimely death of her father in 1938 at the age of 43, when John was only 12. Harold was a strict and humorless disciplinarian who insisted that the kids follow his rules. Typical of his authority and parsimony was his strict rationing of butter. Ted, who was the most defiant of the Penton children, once angrily announced at the dinner table, "When I grow up and get rich, I'm going to eat all the butter I want!"

After Harold's death, Nina, who raised the children on her own and lived to the age of 87, took a less strict and more understanding approach to rearing the family. Ike, Ted, and Hank were the elder males. They had already matured under the strict upbringing of their father, and it fell upon them to help manage the family business. Mary, the middle child, was the eldest daughter and played a strong domestic role, working in the market and helping her mother with household chores.

The young Pentons, circa 1943. Left to right: Bill, Pat, Ike, mother Nina Musselman Penton, Ted, Mary, Hank, and John (Penton family photo).

John, Pat, and Bill, still kids in their formative years, found themselves with more liberty and less supervision.

Pat explains why this is important in understanding the development of John's leadership skills and his dominant personality: "It was like two separate groups of kids, like two families in sequence. John always admired Ted and was very close to him. But it was not as though John were just a little brother to Ted and the older boys. John was more like the leader of the second segment of the family—the big brother to Bill and me."

Patricia and Bill idolized John and were inseparable from him. Patricia continues, "Bill and I would get up early and follow John around and try to help with whatever he was doing. He had muskrat traps and we would go with him to check his traps. We would pick blackberries and bittersweet with him. In the spring we had to cut the asparagus every morning before school. We would get up at five to help John. He would cut and Bill and I would carry. John would cultivate the melon field with a horse-drawn plow. Bill and I would run ahead and move the melon vines. Whatever John did, we were happy to help with. And he would look after us. He never left us behind. He had a bicycle and we would all pile on. I would sit on the handlebars and Bill would sit on the crossbar while John pedaled us down the road."

Early on, John exhibited the athletic skill and risk-taking ability that would one day characterize his approach to business and his reputation as a world-class off-road motorcyclist. Pat states, "At the age of eight, John was the king of the old sandstone quarries where we went swimming. There was one ledge that was 60 feet above the water, and John was the only kid who would dive from that ledge. He was legendary among other kids all over town." Ted added, "He could swim the farthest and the fastest of anyone who ever challenged him, either on top or beneath the water. Many local football fans remember him as a plucky little quarterback."

At 5' 5" and 155 pounds, John was his high school's quarterback for three years, and for a period of time held the school pole vaulting record. Maybe even then, John had begun to understand the importance of better materials and technology, which he would one day pursue in the design of his motorcycles. John states, "I held the record when we used bamboo poles. When high-tech vaulting poles came in, my record went out the window." John believes he would have become an athletic coach had he not been so badly bitten by the motorcycle bug. Doug Wilford, an Amherst resident who eventually went to work for the Pentons, says, "John was a skilled and determined athlete. If it had not been for the timing of the war, I think he could have become some kind of individual Olympic champion."

Due to a variety of circumstances, most of the Penton men did not see active duty during the second world war. Hank had been born with a club foot. Ted had lost an eye in a tree-pruning accident. Bill was still too young for the draft. And, following the death of Harold, Ike had become the male head of the household. Having been raised around ships at the port of Lorain, Ohio, John signed up for the Merchant Marine in 1943. Following a period of moving iron ore on the Great Lakes from

Duluth to Cleveland, John heard rumors that the lake sailors were going to be drafted. He went to the War Shipping Administration in Cleveland and signed up for the Merchant Marine Maritime Service so he could go to sea.

If this was intended to keep him out of someone's gun sights, it proved an unsuccessful plan. John immediately shipped out of Norfolk, Virginia, aboard a freighter carrying bombs and war supplies to Murmansk, Russia. All told, he made three round trip Atlantic crossings during a period when the German U-boats were hunting in wolf packs. During one crossing, half the convoy was sent to the bottom. Shuttling troops and supplies from Algiers to Brendisi, Italy, was no less hazardous. John says, "While we were in port at Brendisi, we were bombed by German planes based just across the Adriatic in Yugoslavia. They sank 22 ships. No one even remembers it today, but it was the second-most destructive harbor bombing in history, second only to Pearl Harbor."

After a year and a half of being a sitting duck aboard a Liberty Ship, John returned home to Amherst. He reports, "I was in the house for about two hours when the FBI called. They wanted to know if I would come talk to them, or if they should come and arrest me." John voluntarily went to an interview with the FBI and learned that they considered him a draft dodger. He showed them all of his maritime papers, proving that he had been in the service of his country. They said, "Well, maybe you're not a draft dodger after all, but you need to go report to your local draft board." There, John found a decidedly unsympathetic reception. He showed the board his papers and explained he had been getting shot at frequently by Germans for the last year or so. It was all to no avail. John says, "I'll never forget it. The chairwoman's name was Sadie Dick, and she said to me, "None of you Penton boys have gone in the service, and you're going to go! End of discussion."

During one of their Atlantic crossings, John's freighter had transported 300 soldiers to Algiers in the hold of the ship. Seeing how those troops lived and were forced to endure the crossing, John had long since decided he did not fancy the life of an infantryman. Trusting his experience and luck as a sailor,

John joined the Navy. By now, it was 1945 and his LSM (Landing Ship Medium), sailing out of San Francisco, never caught up with real action, as the war was winding down. They sailed to Hawaii, then to Okinawa. U.S. strategy at that stage of the war was to surround and contain Japan for an imminent invasion, and John's flotilla sailed to Korea, which was still under Japanese occupation. Thanks to the atomic bomb, John's flotilla did not have to enter hostile waters. During the winter of early 1946, they went peacefully ashore in Seoul as the defeated Japanese withdrew.

John sailed home, having earned the rank of Chief Motor Machinist's Mate. From San Diego they traveled through the Panama Canal to Norfolk, where he received his discharge in 1946. Back home in Amherst, he went to work at the shipyards in Lorain. He went to college at Baldwin-Wallace in Berea, Ohio, for a little over a year, but did not complete a degree. After working as an electrician at U.S. Steel for a year, he went to work with his older brothers in Amherst in 1948.

America's great era of highway construction had just begun. The construction of the Interstate highway system and its feeder systems was underway, and the Penton property was not spared. To correct drainage problems caused by the new highways across Lorain County, the Penton brothers started a ditching business. Then they opened a small machine shop on North Ridge Road, primarily to keep their own excavating and ditching equipment in working order. Ike and Ted became highly skilled machinists, and this venture eventually figured prominently in John's future contribution to the motorcycle industry, becoming the development center for the motorcycles that carried the Penton name.

3

The Penton Brothers Become
Motorcycle Dealers

John Penton mustered out of the Navy with $600 in his pocket, and he wanted a motorcycle. However, new motorcycles were in short supply following the war. To improve his chances, he placed a $100 deposit with each of four different northern Ohio Harley-Davidson dealers. Two years later he still did not have his new motorcycle, so in 1948 he settled for and rebuilt a used, 61-cubic inch Harley-Davidson Knucklehead.

Bill had purchased a 45-cubic inch military surplus Harley WLA in 1947. He entered it that year in the legendary Jack Pine Enduro in Michigan. An enduro is an off-road motorcycling competition over natural, rough terrain. In the eastern United States it may be called a "mud run" when there are especially wet and difficult riding conditions. Although many enthusiasts refer to it as a "race," in actuality, an enduro is more like a timed rally. Riders are expected to proceed along a prescribed route at a particular average speed, usually in the neighborhood of 25 miles per hour. At various checkpoints along the course, they must stop to have their progress recorded. It is a sophisticated and intelligent form of competition, because riders lose points for being either early or late at a checkpoint. They must ride hard, but not too fast, because arriving early at a checkpoint will reduce their score. A rider is disqualified if he is an hour late, or if he deviates from the course to try to make up lost time. Each rider begins the event with 1,000 points, from which his errors are deducted, and the rider who finishes with the highest score wins. Enduros can range from 50 to several hundred miles in length. The Jack Pine Enduro, one of the most difficult in America, was a 500-mile event lasting two days.

Bill did not finish the 1947 Jack Pine, but in 1948, both he and John rode their motorcycles to Michigan to enter the event. John did not finish either, but he remembers Aub LeBard motoring past him on a British BSA. In that era, many riders still believed that the wide tires of a Harley-Davidson were necessary to traverse the Jack Pine's sandy terrain. Seeing LeBard's performance aboard the new British "lightweight" with its relatively narrow tires caused John to question conventional wisdom. In 1949, he returned to the Jack Pine with a B33 BSA and finished second. Only one point separated him from Michigan Harley-Davidson dealer Bert Cummings, but he was elated to finish one point ahead of another famous Harley dealer, Earl Robinson. This near victory only whetted John's appetite to win the Jack Pine. He would finish second several times over the next few years, but it would be another nine years before he achieved his victory.

Following the 1948 Jack Pine, Ike, Ted, John, and Bill formed the Penton Brothers Motorcycle Agency, turning a converted chicken coop next to their machine shop on North Ridge Road into a motorcycle dealership for BSA motorcycles. "We called up American BSA chief Alfred Child and said we wanted to become dealers. He sold us two new BSAs and we were in business," John said. Penton Bros. became incorporated on July 2, 1951.

Although the enterprise was a partnership of the four brothers, by this time Bill was running the family farm and Ike was managing the machine shop. John and Ted focused their attention on becoming motorcycle dealers. Truthfully, the Penton boys were like many dealers of the era. They went into business to support their own two-wheeled habits and get their parts at wholesale. It was not uncommon for dealers in the 1950s to have nothing but used motorcycles on the floor, having

The Penton brothers in 1950, left to right: Bill, Ted, John, and Ike (Penton family photo).

ridden or raced all of their new stock before offering it for sale to their customers.

By the late 1950s, motorcycling had begun to take off in America, the Pentons and other dealers were beginning to prosper, and motorcycling was becoming more highly organized. On a cold evening during the winter of 1953, John, Ted, and eight of their motorcycling buddies were hanging out and bench racing in the warmth of the Penton machine shop. It became obvious they had the makings of a club, and on that basis they formed a non-profit association and purchased 38 acres of land on Crosse Road, west of Amherst. One day, while surveying the wooded property for plans to build a race track and a clubhouse, someone noted the frequent call of singing birds and said, "Hey, let's call ourselves the Meadowlarks." They

When it's too cold to ride, the Meadowlarks sing. Left to right: Elmer Reichert, Bill Clever, John Penton, Bob Knapp at the piano, and Dave Ray, circa 1954 (Penton family photo).

incorporated their club on November 17, 1954, and the Amherst Meadowlarks Motorcycle Club grew from the original ten members to more than forty over the next three years. The American Motorcyclist Association chartered it and they built a race track and a 2,000-square foot clubhouse on the land, complete with a fireplace and banquet facilities. Ted and John both served as trustees for the club, and John was president for seven years. The Amherst Meadowlarks remains a prominent motorcycle club today, one of the leading providers of organized motorcycling activity in northern Ohio.

Over the years, the Penton dealership handled an array of brands, including Husqvarna, KTM, Penton, CZ, BSA, BMW, Ariel, Matchless, NSU, Zundapp, and every Japanese brand with the exception of Kawasaki. By 1961, the "chicken coop" was selling 200 Hondas a year, in addition to other brands, and in 1962 the brothers built an attractive, modern facility on Cooper-Foster Road on the north frontage of the Penton farm. For appearance, space, and style, it ranked favorably against

John Penton at NSU service school, 1958 (Penton family photo).

any motorcycle dealership of the era. It had terrazzo floors, piped-in music, a 1,200-square foot showroom with floor-to-ceiling glass on three sides, tiled restrooms, and a separate service department with hydraulic lifts.

With stronger sales, the Pentons staffed their larger operation by hiring Kathie Staschick (soon to become Kathie Towne) and Elmer Towne (called Towney), Elmer Reichert, and Ralph Haslage. Kathie sold parts and accessories, did title work, and handled the accounting. Towney and Ralph ran the service department, and Reichert helped with sales and general management. Kathie recalls that John was the Penton brother most frequently involved in the retail business. John confirms that by this time, the Penton machine shop had acquired some good subcontracts from Nordson for Defense Department production, and Ted was spending a lot of time there, assisting Ike. About his role at the dealership, John laughs, "I wasn't very good on the sales floor. Instead of just closing the deal and selling a motorcycle, I would start telling people all of the ways the motorcycle could be improved, talking down my own products without realizing it." Of course, it was this vocal passion for a better motorcycle that eventually caused others to challenge John to either shut up or build a better motorcycle—a challenge he would one day accept.

Kathie Towne recalls those days: "It was a fun business then. Working was fun. There was a lot of variety and we enjoyed what we were doing. Guys hung around and bench raced. It wasn't just a dealership; it was a social center. There were a lot of good years at Penton Brothers." Today, the dealership still carries the Penton name but is no longer owned by the family. It sells Honda, Suzuki, and KTM motorcycles, snowmobiles, and personal watercraft, and has expanded to four times its original floor space. Owned by Dale Barris, it is a spit-and-polish operation with a modern service department and a wide line of clothing and accessories. High on a shelf around the interior, special motorcycles create a kind of mini-museum: an early Husqvarna, a mint-condition Honda scrambler, a near-perfect Honda step-through Cub, and most remarkable of all, the 1968 Penton #V001, the first serial production motorcycle to carry the Penton name. Today it is owned by local resident and long-time Penton family friend, Norm Miller, who located, rescued, and restored it in 1995.

Characteristically, John Penton built his businesses around members of his family. When the large Penton family could not provide the talent and manpower to fill key slots in the growing Penton enterprise, John simply created an extended family. John would handpick young, enthusiastic people, become their mentor, give them opportunities, and engender in them a kind of family-like loyalty that has prevailed over the years, through good times and bad. Many who moved on, sometimes through difficult and unfortunate downsizing, never got far away from John, physically or emotionally.

Although Barris' business is no longer connected with the Penton family in any way, he can be seen as a member of this extended family. Dale, who is one year younger than John's son Jack, was raised in the Amherst area and raced motocross and rode enduros with the Penton boys. He worked for the Penton motorcycle dealership in 1970, setting up new motorcycles and working in the parts department.

By the mid-1970s, the retail motorcycle business in the United States started a major and lengthy downward trend, hammered by rising prices, unfavorable international currency exchange rates, environmental criticism, and growing government regulation. During that period, Barris worked at other dealerships in the area and eventually moved to Atlanta where he worked at the dealership of former motocross champion Bryan Kenney. In October 1986 he ran into John at an annual motorcycle rally near Atlanta and asked him if he was interested in selling the retail business. To Barris' surprise, John confided that the dealership was not doing well, that his time was fully occupied with other business issues, and that, in fact, it was his intention to close the store for good on January 1, 1987.

Barris returned to Amherst between Christmas and the new year to negotiate for the dealership. John financed the sale, but gave him poor odds for survival. He said, "I don't think you'll make it two years." Nevertheless, the deal was consummated with a handshake, rather than a contract, and Barris took over the operation in February, 1987. It is doubtful that John would have struck such a deal with someone he did not consider a member of his extended family.

One of the sticking points in the deal was the Penton name. John did not want it to remain on a dealership not controlled by the family, but Barris considered it essential to his success. He says, "I think John had no concept of the power of that name. He's probably right that the shop would not have survived if I had let him take away the Penton name." Barris continues, "We're still known as a dirt-bike shop. Although the Penton motorcycle is long gone, people still come here to buy Hondas and KTMs because of the Penton legacy. They come here and ask me about John and whether he ever comes into the shop. I tell them he wanders in and out all the time." He says with a laugh, "A lot of them still think John owns the shop, and they can't believe that to us, he's just another local guy who comes around."

Barris looks thoughtful and concludes, "You know, it's just been in recent years that John has begun to figure out that he's a celebrity. He really likes it that his name is still on the shop and that people come around here hoping to get a look at him. It has really worked out well for everyone."

John admits that he loves to walk down the hill from his house on North Ridge, wander around the dealership, and listen to the customers. He marvels at what the motorcycle business has become and how it has changed from the chicken coop next to the machine shop from which he and his brothers launched their retail agency. He shakes his head in disbelief and says, "I saw this young couple come in and buy their son a new KTM minicycle and all the best fancy riding gear with a credit card. Boy, it wasn't like that in my day!"

John can look out over his front lawn today to see the dealership he calls the "chicken coop" on the south side of North Ridge Road. He can look out his back window to see the business started by him and his three brothers in 1950, a thriving concern that still carries their name. Separated by only a few hundred feet, it is a long, long distance from one to the other in time and significance. Owning a motorcycle dealership would have been enough for many enthusiasts. For John it was not. Eventually, he would feel compelled to build the motorcycles that would be sold through Penton Brothers and 300 other dealerships throughout America.

4

A Tragic Test for the Penton Family

Patricia Penton had a college friend from Chardon, Ohio, named Katherine Marks who came to live with her while she took a summer job in Amherst. John and Katherine began to date and were married on June 26th, 1949. Over the next five years they had three sons: Tom was born on May 19, 1950; Jeff on April 15, 1952; and Jack on July 16, 1954.

In early 1957, Katherine was diagnosed with primary progressive multiple sclerosis. She became blind within a week of the diagnosis and went rapidly downhill. John was overwhelmed, trying to help Ted run the motorcycle dealership, dealing with three small boys—Jack was only two years old—and caring for a tragically ill and dying wife. But the family pitched in. Aunt Pat, whose son Dane was the same age as Jeff, took Jeff in. Aunt Mary took Tom. Uncle Ike took Jack.

Pat says about the situation, "We were always a tribal bunch. Aunts and uncles all over the place, and kids staying with their cousins for days at a time. I don't think the boys even thought it was something unusual." She continues, "But for the rest of us it was a terrible year, and a terrible strain on John. He was deeply in love with Katherine, and it was so sad for her. The day we decided to take the boys to the other households, she cried and said, 'They took my baby's crib down today.' She was blind, but she knew what was going on." Years later in an article in *Motorcyclist,* Ted added, "There isn't a more heartbreaking loss any man could possibly endure than to watch the young mother of his three husky sons wither away to death. He nursed her with a tenderness that was almost a prayer, and nobody who watched him in that vigil would question the depth of this man's goodness."

Katherine Penton died on February 28th, 1958. John was shattered. He says, "I was totally broken up, but I was also relieved that her ordeal had ended. I didn't know how I felt. My life had totally changed and I think I was kind of insane." John handled his grief and confusion by asking the family to continue to keep the boys, and he threw himself into a year of remarkable, frenetic motorcycling exploits and achievements.

He began the year by winning the Ohio State Enduro Championship, his last victory aboard a BSA. Next he rode to Daytona, and on the way he stopped in Georgia and won the Stone Mountain Enduro using the 175cc NSU motorcycle he was riding on the road. From there he rode to Florida, entering and winning the Alligator Enduro with the same motorcycle. Returning to Ohio, he rode to and won the Little Burr Enduro,

John Penton, his 175cc NSU, and his future ISDT Trophy Team, left to right: Jeff, Jack, and Tom in 1958 (Penton family photo).

then the Jack Pine, then the Corduroy Enduro in Canada. In every case he rode to and from the event on the same 175cc NSU he used to win. Not only did he ride hundreds of miles to and from the events, he became notorious for drafting trucks and Greyhound buses, tucking in just inches behind the rear of the large vehicles to gain speed. He opined that he liked buses better because they did not kick up so much dirt and debris.

Following his Corduroy victory, John mounted a BMW R69 and headed west, then into Mexico for a month. He lived on the road and slept on the ground next to his motorcycle, laying the BMW over on one cylinder and throwing a canvas over it to create a makeshift tent. John laughs, "One morning I awoke to many voices chattering in Spanish all around me. I crawled out and realized I had bedded down right in the middle of a footpath used by the local villagers. They probably thought I had crashed there and was dead!" He adds, "Man, I was really on the bum. I'm not sure what I was doing, or why I was doing it. I just needed to keep riding to try to figure out what had happened to me."

It was late in the year and the nights in Mexico were cold, especially as John gained elevation as he rode toward Mexico City. He relates, "One night I stopped at an old service station just as they were closing up. I just huddled there by the stove and shook and looked pitiful. They didn't speak a word of English and I didn't speak a word of Spanish, but somehow they figured out I had no place to stay, so they just locked the place up and left me inside. The next morning when they opened up, I thanked them and was on my way."

Near Mexico City, John met an American who told him it was warmer in Acapulco. John had never heard of the place, but if it was warm, that's where he wanted to go. There he saw the famous cliff divers. John says, "I recalled diving in the Amherst quarries, and I figured I could do that. But I realized I wasn't a teenager anymore, so I chickened out." It was one of the few times that John's good judgment overcame the appeal of a good challenge.

From Mexico's Pacific coast he headed north toward California. Once back in the United States, he decided it was time to return home, and that return was to be as spectacular as all of his 1958 motorcycling exploits. He rode straight through to Amherst, nonstop. He and his brothers had read about the transcontinental record runs of the legendary Cannonball Baker, and after John showed he could cross more than half the country without rest, Ted, who called John "Slug," said, "Well, Slug, why don't you just go out there and break that record." It was a challenge that John could not resist.

In the spring of 1959 he began to train and make plans for a transcontinental record attempt. According to long-time friend Al Born, John trained for the record attempt by illegally entering the Ohio Turnpike through a culvert and a hole in the fence along the tollway. He would roar from one end of the turnpike to the other endlessly, then exit back into Amherst through the hole in the fence without having to pay a toll or create a record that would reveal his illegal speeds.

Left to right: John Penton, *Cycle Magazine* publisher Floyd Clymer, and AMA official Earl Flanders following John's transcontinental record run in 1959 (Penton family photo).

John Penton, following his transcontinental record run in 1959 (Penton family photo).

Cycle Magazine publisher Floyd Clymer congratulates John after his 1959 transcontinental record run. The motorcycle: a 1959 BMW R69 (Penton family photo).

Early in June, John took up the challenge, departing for New York aboard his BMW R69 outfitted with a large fuel tank. After a day of rest as a guest of the U.S. BMW distributor Alfred Bondy, John recorded his time and location with Western Union, pointed his wheel westward, and set out for California on June 8th, stopping only for fuel, water, and candy bars. Fifty-two hours, eleven minutes, and one second later, he checked in with Western Union in Los Angeles. He had covered 3,051 miles at an average speed of just over 58 miles per hour. He complained that his record run was flawed by a 45-minute rest near Albuquerque, and John reported at the end of the ride, "Everything got real hazy and I began to see double." Then he said, "All I want right now is some sleep."

The record run turned John into a motorcycling legend. BMW featured it prominently in its advertising. Newspapers all over the world reported it. Five years later when John went to Europe to compete in the ISDT, everyone knew his name. People from as far away as Czechoslovakia shook his hand and said they had read about him in their local newspapers.

During his stay in California following the record run, John paid a visit to an old Ohio motorcycling buddy named Bob Hochenedel, his wife Donna, and their two daughters and one son. Bob, like John, was a member of the Amherst Meadowlarks Motorcycle Club, and he had continued his racing career after moving to California, entering weekly flat track races at the famous Ascot race track in Gardena. During a late evening conversation with Bob and Donna, John said, "Hokey, why the hell don't you quit this motorcycle racing at Ascot. You've got a wife and three kids and one of these days you're going to kill yourself." Bob laughed, "John, if I kill myself racing motorcycles I want you to take Donna and the kids back to Ohio and take care of them with all the social security money." John finished his visit and rode his BMW back to Ohio. Within a month, Bob Hochenedel was dead, killed in a crash at Ascot. Personal loss continued to dog John Penton, but the untimely death of Bob Hochenedel would have a profound and ultimately beneficial affect on the Penton family.

Following her husband's death, Donna and her children returned to Elyria, Ohio, where they had lived before their move to California. Elyria is about ten miles from Amherst, and John and Donna began to see each other. Donna had met John only once before his California visit, at a New Year's Eve party put on by the Amherst Meadowlarks. But they now had a lot in common, each trying to raise young families following the untimely death of a spouse.

Donna says, "I had three kids and was not occupationally trained. How was I going to raise three kids? John had three small boys with no mother. John and I were dating and we thought it would be a good idea to bring the families together. Another reason I married John was because Bob thought so much of him. John was my husband's hero." John and Donna held their wedding reception at the Amherst Meadowlarks Club House.

Tragedy for two families had resulted in a new and grander Penton clan consisting of Tom, 10; Jeff, 8; Laura, 8; Jack, 6; Barbara, 5; and Brad, 3. The blended family moved into a tiny

The third generation: the Penton/Hochenedel blended family. Left to right: Barbara and Brad Hochenedel, Tom holding Tim Penton, Laura Hochenedel, and Jeff and Jack Penton (Penton family photo).

house on the Penton farm, a house so small that all of the kids had to sleep in an attic divided by curtains into a boys' side and a girls' side. The situation became even more crowded when John and Donna had a seventh child, Tim, in 1961. In 1963 John built the house in which he and Donna still live today. Donna says about those first three years, "It was a challenge, but I would rather be busy than lonely."

But deep personal loss was not over for John and Donna Penton. At nine years of age, young Brad died in his mother's arms from complications following a playground accident. At the age of 21, cousin Teddy Leimbach, one of the most promising off-road riders in the Penton clan, was killed in a freak automobile accident in Lorain in 1980. Donna still tears up as she recalls the deaths: "We've lost Pat's husband Paul. Ted, Bill, and Hank are gone. John really looked up to Ted. And Bill, who was very easygoing, could handle John better than anyone in the family. He understood John and could give advice in ways John would accept. He had a dog named Felix who was always with him in his pickup. I still look out the back window and think it is about time to see Bill and his red truck coming up the driveway. We really miss all of them."

Ted had to stop riding motorcycles before his death, due to head injuries suffered in a street-riding motorcycle accident. Long-time extended family member Norm Miller talks about him: "John drove the business, but Ted was the people person. He could get along with God and Satan at the same time. Ted gave me my first motorcycle ride in 1958 on his BMW when I was five years old. I gave Ted his last motorcycle ride on my Harley. Ted was really sad when he could no longer ride motorcycles. I would come by and he would get on the buddy seat behind me. He really loved getting out and feeling the wind."

John Penton is known to many as a self-reliant person. But again and again, throughout his life, his solutions have come only through the strength of family. It is sadly logical that large families suffer more losses, but the Pentons have always made it through and solved their problems by relying upon one another. From the original seven of John's generation have come twenty children and 45 grandchildren . . . so far.

5

The Jack Pine Challenge

The 500-mile, two-day Jack Pine Enduro, run out of Lansing, Michigan, was considered by many the most prestigious off-road motorcycling event in the United States. For serious enduro riders it was the paramount challenge, and for many camp followers it was a magical mystery tour. Whole families came to Michigan to watch and support their rider. In a time before abundant motels, locals opened up their homes to provide places to stay. The Lansing Motorcycle Club fed 1,200 people at a time. Many entered without even bothering to get accommodations for the first night, knowing they would be disqualified and on their way home before the start of the second day. All they wanted was to say they had ridden a little bit of the legendary Jack Pine. Riders arrived with anything and everything to have a crack at negotiating the soft Michigan sand. Michigander Larry Maiers, who became Penton Imports' CEO from 1972 to 1984, tried to ride the Jack Pine on a Honda Trail-90. Doug Wilford, who later became a serious and accomplished enduro rider and who worked for John Penton for seven years, entered the Jack Pine at age 16 aboard a Whizzer!

After John Penton finished second—just one point behind winner Burt Cummings—on only his second try in 1949, the Jack Pine pretty much became his obsession. About their annual Jack Pine preparation Ted said, "You didn't need a calendar in our neighborhood to tell when September was approaching, for by the first week in August the lights in our shop burned later each night. It was as common as the summer

John and Donna with his NSU and trophies from the Jack Pine, the Corduroy, and other championship enduros, 1960 (Penton family photo).

Young champions: Bill and John on their BSAs, circa 1950 (Penton family photo).

breeze to be awakened in the night by the explosion of a highly-tuned engine."

John's competitive edge may have been sharpened by the fact that younger brother Bill won the event in 1954. While winning the famous cow bell trophy was important to John Penton, his real obsession with the Jack Pine was how he used it, year after year, as a laboratory in his quest to find the ultimate enduro motorcycle. Early on, he doubted the conventional wisdom that one needed wide tires and lots of power to survive in the sandy terrain. These doubts would lead him down a path of experimentation that eventually resulted in a motorcycle of his own making.

Spurning the size and weight of the Harley-Davidson he had ridden in 1948, Penton tried a BSA for several years. It was a B33 BSA that brought him a second place in 1949 and

John Penton, his family, and national championship enduro trophies in 1960. Left to right are John, Donna, Jack, Laura, Brad, Tom, Jeff, and Barbara. Tim was born a year later. John is holding his coveted Jack Pine trophy and Jack is holding a Jack Pine cow bell (Jerry West photo).

John Penton on his NSU Maxi at the finish line of the Jack Pine, 1958 (Penton family photo).

The winning combination of John and his 1958 NSU, complete with art deco fender ornament (Penton family photo).

caused the Penton brothers to open a motorcycle dealership. But the BSA's electrical system was not always reliable, and it could take on water through its open-throated carburetors. Sucking water into a running internal combustion engine has disastrous results, causing a condition known as "hydro-locking" that will instantly destroy internal parts. Consequently, riders had to have the ingenuity and mechanical skill to extensively modify motorcycles designed for the street, such as the BSA, in order to make them safe and reliable for enduro competition. As far as John was concerned, he had not yet found the ideal off-road competition machine in his B33 BSA.

Penton Brothers took on a franchise for the German-made NSU in 1957. John and Ted studied the NSU engine and considered it a marvelous, well-constructed design. It had an overhead cam driven by an unconventional system of eccentric cranks that came straight out of the company's history as a

John, Donna, Brad, and Barbara with John's NSU enduro bike and trophies from the Jack Pine, the Corduroy, and other championship enduros, 1960 (Penton family photo).

John Penton, holding his trophy after winning the 1961 Alligator Enduro
(Daytona International Speedway photo).

John Penton
with his NSU
and trophy from
the Little Burr,
1961 (Jerry West
photo).

John Penton, his 250cc BMW, and his Little Burr trophy in 1962. In the foreground is the Schulyer County enduro trophy (Jerry West photo).

John Penton (BMW) and Owen Christman (BSA) prepare to depart for a 200-mile enduro at Southwick, Massachusetts, in 1962 (Boyd Reynolds, Action Sports photo).

John Penton aboard his BMW at the 1963 Sandy Lane enduro (Boyd Reynolds, Action Sports photo).

sewing machine manufacturer. This engine was beautifully machined to close tolerances and produced good power for its weight and size. The motorcycle also had a robust, pressed metal frame into which its carburetor was vented through a waterproof rubber tube. While NSU offered 125, 175, and 250cc models, John chose the 175 because its power-to-weight ratio was the best of the three. Setting up an NSU for the 1958 season, John turned in a storming performance, winning Stone Mountain, Alligator, Little Burr, Jack Pine, and the Corduroy, which was the Canadian national championship. He won the Little Burr on it in 1959, and rode it to victories at the Jack Pine, Sandy Lane, Corduroy, and Ball and Chain Enduros in 1960. He scored on it again at Little Burr in 1962, then switched to a BMW for another victory at the Corduroy.

John Penton aboard his 250cc BMW at the 1964 Sandy Lane enduro (Boyd Reynolds, Action Sports photo).

The switch came because NSU was going out of the motorcycle business, and it was unlikely that parts would be available much longer. John also liked the reliability of BMW motorcycles, for which Penton Brothers had taken a franchise in 1952. He figured its fully-enclosed drive shaft would preclude the possibility of chain wear and failure. Besides, the single-cylinder R27 had its carburetor vented through a rubber tube into an air box which, with a little care and preparation, could guard against water intake. One disadvantage was the motorcycle's heavy, cumbersome Earls forks, so John installed lighter and more conventional Ariel forks.

After the season-ending victory at the Corduroy in 1961, John rode the BMW to victories at Little Burr, Sandy Lane, and Schuyler County, New York, in 1962. These performances got the attention of the Munich-based factory, which sponsored John to ride the motorcycle at the International Six Days' Trial that year. This experience would start a new chapter in John's motorcycling career, and open doors that would lead to the

John Penton, displaying his 1967 Jack Pine trophy (Boyd Reynolds, Action Sports photo).

creation of his own motorcycle. But prior to the arrival of the Penton, John would ride the little Beemer to another Jack Pine victory in 1964.

Notable about his enduro motorcycles is the fact that in every case John chose a smaller engine from the available options. He picked the 12.5 horsepower 175cc Maxi NSU over the more powerful 250cc Sport Max. While BMW had 500cc and 600cc models in its product line, Penton chose the little 250cc with only 18 horsepower. His philosophy that smaller may be better was taking shape, and it would eventually become a central concept in the design of the Penton motorcycle.

In 1967, the Pentons were invited to become the distributor for the Swedish Husqvarna motorcycle for the 38 eastern states, and with the arrival of the Husky, America's off-road motorcycle revolution was well under way. Here was, at last, a serial production vehicle that did not have to be drastically

John Penton
aboard his
Husqvarna in
1969,
demonstrating
why easterners
call it "mud
running" (Boyd
Reynolds, Action
Sports photo).

modified for off-road use. In fact, it was designed solely for that purpose and was not suitable as a road bike. It was light, lean, tough, and had a responsive two-stroke engine. Penton got his final Jack Pine victory aboard a Husqvarna in 1967.

Pursuing his belief that power could be sacrificed in favor of lightness and agility, Penton began to immediately lobby the Husqvarna factory to produce a 125cc motorcycle. Husqvarna already had a 175cc engine, and John believed it could easily be stroked down and updated as a high-performance 125. But they disagreed. Their standard models were 250 and 360cc, and in fact it was their intention to go larger, not smaller. They had no faith in Penton's belief that smaller could be better, and their refusal to consider his request only stimulated John Penton's desire to find a way to build his own off-road dream machine.

It was an idea that had been taking shape for at least five years. Several times John had said to his colleagues, "I can remember every part that ever broke on my motorcycles during an enduro. I guess the only thing to do is take all of the best parts from different motorcycles and put them together." But John would have been satisfied to take an easier path. Today he says, "I never wanted to become an importer. If Husky had just built that little 125, the Penton motorcycle would never have been created. It was their own stubbornness that brought a competing brand into the market."

The original seed that grew into the Penton motorcycle may have been planted in 1962 during an exchange between Penton and Triumph representative Jack Mercer. Mercer had been trying for some time to get Penton Brothers to sell Triumph motorcycles. John believed the market was moving beyond the quality and style that Triumph had to offer, and besides, the dealership already carried its British-built rival, BSA. One day, as Mercer continued to press his case, Penton described in great detail everything he thought wrong with the Triumph. Completely exasperated, Mercer replied, "If you know so damned much about designing motorcycles, why don't you just go build your own?"

John and Jack Mercer remained lifelong friends, but John Penton always was a sucker for a challenge.

6

Penton Publishing

Through the 1950s, motorcycle journalism in America consisted of three magazines: *Cycle, Motorcyclist,* and *American Motorcycling. Cycle* and *Motorcyclist* were the only two commercial publications. *American Motorcycling* (later to be renamed *AMA News,* then subsequently *American Motorcyclist*) was the house organ of the American Motorcyclist Association and was available only to AMA members. All three viewed motorcycling from a strictly national perspective. All behaved as if motorcycling ended at the boundaries of the United States, providing little or no information about racing in other parts of the world. Although *American Motorcycling* published a monthly calendar of local events and the point standings for amateur racers on a quarterly basis, none of the three provided significant news coverage about local events.

Their editorial policies were probably driven more by tradition and habit than by any thought-out strategy. Much of the information published came from news releases which were unedited—set in type just as they had fallen out of the envelope. Product photographs were stock studio shots provided by the manufacturers. When action pictures appeared, they were often the grainy snapshots from an amateur photographer's Brownie. Editorially, these magazines were emblems of the isolationist policies that had been established by the motorcycle industry as early as 1924, and representative of a status quo mentality that remained unchallenged for forty years.

The first journalist to break out of the pattern was Joe Parkhurst, who, with his wife Betty Jean, founded *Cycle World* in 1962. Parkhurst had worked for John Bond whose *Road & Track* had shown him what could be accomplished with good editing, real road tests, investigative journalism, professional photography, and excitingly written reports about racing events all over the world. *Road & Track* became his model for a new motorcycle journalism that provided an opportunity for American readers to get information beyond the limited scope provided by the long-standing Big Three. For motorcyclists, it became part of the milieu of revolution that was sweeping America in the 1960s. *Cycle World's* new direction was well characterized by its December 1962 cover, which depicted John Penton aboard his BMW R27 at the ISDT in Germany. None of *Cycle World's* competitors would have been likely to report on an international event, much less depict it on the cover.

For a period of time, a young California journalist named Chuck Clayton worked at *Cycle World*. Clayton understood the potential of Parkhurst's new approach, but was dissatisfied with the lack of timeliness inherent in a monthly publication. Clayton believed in the commercial viability of news promptly delivered, and decided there was enough news on the booming motorcycling scene to justify a weekly tabloid newspaper. He and his wife Sharon set up C&S Publishing in September 1965 and purchased a small local motorcycling tabloid named *Motorcycle Journal* that had existed in the southern California market for about a year. Within two months, they'd changed the name to *Cycle News* and expanded coverage to provide information on both local and national events. The Claytons also installed in *Cycle News* a social and political conscience, reporting and editorializing on the new laws and regulations that had begun to affect motorcycling. *Cycle News* strove to stimulate grass roots activism among rank and file motorcyclists, something not pursued by any other publication of the day. The venture broke new ground, requiring new techniques of timely distribution, which were worked out and mastered by the Claytons by 1967. *Cycle News* became a going concern. Believing they had discovered a winning formula, the Claytons began to talk about launching a sister publication in the eastern United States.

In the meantime, John Penton was back East demonstrating that his great uncle John Augustus was not the only Penton interested in publishing. Seeing the need for timely coverage of the local cycling scene, Penton launched a little tabloid in 1967 called *State Motorcycle News.* It was a genuine good-of-the-sport venture, not just a vehicle to promote Penton motorcycles, since Penton motorcycles had not yet arrived. It was begun as a service to Ohio clubs and riders, to publicize a calendar of events and report on the results of races. Kathie Towne explains, "We started producing it right at Penton Brothers, working after hours. We typed up the information and did pasteups in the evenings. When we didn't have enough information, we just used more pictures." Towne also handled circulation, which grew to about 800 readers within the first year.

But producing a newspaper was a lot more difficult than John had anticipated. It did not take long for him to realize that gathering and editing news, laying out a paper, selling ads, and getting it all printed and posted on a timely basis could be a time-consuming, headache-making task. Some of his own writings in early issues apologized to readers for delays and errors, and commiserated about the unexpectedly tough struggle of the publishing process.

In 1967 the Claytons flew to Ohio for an AMA meeting. On the airplane they talked about how to research the eastern cycling scene to determine whether another publication would be viable. One of the first things their research turned up was the existence of *State Motorcycle News.* John Penton had beat them to the punch, but in their conversations with him they learned that all he wanted was to help motorcycling. He never intended to become a full-time commercial publisher. John and Chuck stayed in touch, feeling one another out on areas of mutual interest.

In 1968 C&S Publishing purchased *State Motorcycle News,* which would become the springboard for their plan to launch *Cycle News East.* Sharon Clayton says, "Money was never an issue. All John Penton wanted was to make sure that local motorcycling continued to get good news coverage. I think he sold the business to us for less than $1,000." She laughs, "It was more like an adoption procedure than a business acquisition. John made us stay at his house and meet his family. It was pretty clear he was trying to decide whether we were the kind of people who would give his paper a good home and make it healthy." As Sharon describes how John handled negotiations, it becomes clear that this was another classic example of his attitude toward business. John Penton was not so much selling a business as he was adopting the Claytons into his extended Penton family.

Because the venture was going to require close attention, Chuck decided to temporarily move back to Ohio to run the operation personally. He didn't even have a desk for his little office in a converted garage on Church Street in Amherst, and asked John where he could get one. John showed him a used desk and said, "This desk is worth $1,000. You can use it for free, but if you let this publication fail you have to pay me for the desk." Chuck had his desk, and no money ever changed hands.

The successful launch of *Cycle News East* meant that its western counterpart could no longer be viewed as just a regional tabloid. News journalism had clearly arrived in the motorcycle industry, and the two sister papers, which delivered skillfully coordinated information, became a powerful axis operation with serious opinion-setting clout. *Cycle News* became a significant cog in the 60s motorcycle revolution. It stimulated interest and created excitement. It changed fundamental marketing strategies throughout the industry, giving businesses an opportunity to advertise ideas and accomplishments while they were fresh and hot, and to target their messages at regional markets. Chuck Clayton's editorials, as well as those of the editors hired by him and Sharon, helped promote reform and greater democracy within the AMA. In support of the AMA's new government relations role in the 70s, *Cycle News* promoted political activism and community conscience. It helped turn up the heat on politicians and bureaucrats who thought they could steamroller motorcycling. It prodded the old guard off their butts and changed motorcycle journalism forever.

As with so many things from that era, John Penton had his hand in the action. *State Motorcycle News* was a humble and short-lived venture, and the Claytons probably would have expanded their publishing empire regardless. But John Penton may have provided the opportunity for it to happen more efficiently and a little more quickly. And, hey, he gave them a desk.

7

The Great Communicator

During his presidency, Ronald Reagan was called "the Great Communicator." His ability to sell, to recruit, to motivate, to engender loyalty, and to change minds came from a tone of voice, a tilt of the head, a kind and empathic smile. The same principles of communication can be seen at work in John Penton. Somehow he can convey his vision and sell concepts through an almost inarticulate delivery of unconnected words and phrases, backed up by ample and extravagant body language and electricity in his eyes.

At first glance, John Penton doesn't come across as a guy who could tell you anything. People who have only heard of the legendary and influential John Penton are invariably astonished when he arrives. He's usually wearing baggy work clothes, what his family and associates call his "green grubbies." His pants are typically held up by suspenders. There will likely be one pant leg rolled calf high for some inexplicable reason, and one white sock so bereft of elastic that it has settled sadly around the top of his shoe, exposing an ankle. Almost everywhere that you see exposed skin on John Penton, you'll find scars from old motorcycle accidents. He appears strong but hard used.

A good physical description of Penton was captured in 1983 by Suzi Mingo, writing for *Dirt Rider* magazine. Mingo wrote of " . . . that mischievous twinkle in those ice-blue eyes, the rebellious cowlick in that iron-grey hair, the raw energy that crackles like static electricity . . . The ears are slightly pointed on top, reminiscent of the mythical Pan. Too-large khaki work clothes constitute his daily attire."

It's that crackling energy that makes others look quickly beyond the packaging to listen to what John Penton has to say. But, again, it's never just what John Penton says. Again, Mingo captured Penton's *modus communicado* when she reported that their interview began with the demand, "Come on, I want to show you something!" That's how John does it. He never says, "Listen up, I want to *tell* you something." He always says, "Come on, I want to *show* you something." Then he's off at a near-run, taking you to see something in a warehouse at Penton Imports, or dumping a chaotic file of papers or photographs on his desk, stirring through them to find whatever it is you need to see. His communication is visual, not verbal.

He communicates with his eyes and his body. He waves his arms like what he's trying to tell you is too frustratingly important to capture with mere words. He rubs his hand over his scalp like he's trying to polish a big thought into greater clarity. His eyes flash with an intensity that leaves you convinced that what's coming next will be truly powerful. At a meeting table, he will raise his hands with palms upward, like he's holding forward an invisible idea. The position of his hands suggests that this idea is surely the size of a Ford van, at least. Quite often the accompanying verbal presentation is downright inarticulate. If you taped it and played it back, it might not make a bit of sense, but in John's presence, the concepts become clear and convincing.

If his spoken words seem inarticulate, the same is not true of his written communication skills. John is a good writer: clear, straightforward, conversational, to the point, and unembellished—skills which became evident in 1967 when he started *State Motorcycle News.* Though publishing and creative writing run through the Penton family (sister Pat is a widely-read columnist and the author of three books, and Ted was published in several motorcycle magazines), John had no personal experience or training in the field. Nevertheless, he threw himself into the project with enthusiasm and a kind of open innocence that gave *State Motorcycle News* a sincere, friendly, fireside quality.

Most issues contained an editorial by John, sometimes delighting in the local motorcycle scene, sometimes admonishing the whole industry for its parochial attitude and lack of support for Americans in international competition. John's vision of motorcycling began to emerge in these writings. That vision, it was clear, encompassed both local and global considerations. It defied limits and ignored boundaries. It lacked prejudice.

There is little doubt that—given a choice—John Penton prefers verbal communication, where he can bring the full force of his personality and animated presence to bear. Through his ability to communicate, he can sell, recruit, motivate, engender loyalty, and change minds. And this is not some slick salesman's technique. Slick, John Penton is not. His great ability to communicate is driven by his powerful conviction that what he envisions is good, important, right, and badly needed. Others don't buy John Penton's ideas. They embrace them.

8

Welcome to the Six Days'

At the age of 22 and just out of the Navy, John Penton's dream was to win the legendary Jack Pine Enduro. By 1962, that desire had sent him on a quest to build a better off-road motorcycle, and earned him two of his four Jack Pine victories. Although he had last won aboard an NSU in 1960, his switch to a BMW near the end of 1961 proved to be one of the most important decisions in his life. His immediate success on the machine got the attention of the BMW factory, which, in that day, was still actively promoting the sporting and performance qualities of its motorcycles. John was invited to come to Garmisch-Partenkirchen, Germany, in September, 1962, to ride the International Six Days' Trial under the sponsorship of the BMW factory.

The ISDT is the most difficult and prestigious off-road motorcycle endurance event on earth, frequently referred to by its followers as the Olympics of motorcycling. It first took place in Great Britain in 1913, and has run annually ever since except when interrupted by world wars. During motorcycling's glory days, when practically every industrialized nation had its own motorcycle industry, the Six Days' was devised as a nationalistic contest to determine whose machines were the best designed and most reliable. National teams competed for two highly prestigious awards: the World Trophy, for six-member teams, and the Silver Vase, for four-member teams. To even ride in the Six Days' is an indication that one is among his nation's best off-road competitors. To host the ISDT means that a nation is recognized among its peers as an off-road motorcycling power. In 1981, the name of the event was modified to the ISDE, the International Six Days' Enduro.

ISDT riders compete on 150 or more miles of difficult trails each day over a period of six consecutive days, trying to maintain a minimum speed, enforced at various points—called "checks" or "controls"—throughout the event. For arriving late at a check, a rider loses points. Although the rules have been modified from time to time over the years, when John Penton was competing, the essence of the event was to test the reliability of the motorcycle as well as the skill and endurance of its rider. No significant repairs were allowed, and no one was permitted to touch the motorcycle except its rider. Fuel and oil could be added, minor adjustments of drive chains and control cables could be made, and tires could be changed, but no other repairs were permissible. Unlike an American enduro, points are not lost for arriving at a check early, so emphasis is placed on speed over challenging terrain. Describing his first Six Days' experience, John Penton said in 1962, "You could call it a pure cross-country race. The idea is to get to the next control early enough to work on the bike." Later he would assert that a

Precious medal: the prize for finishing the International Six Days' Trial (AMA photo).

single day of the ISDT is more difficult than the entire 500-mile Jack Pine Enduro.

While riders must stay on time on the trail, it is also necessary for them to earn bonus points at special tests designed to measure racing—sometimes on pavement—and hill-climbing skills. The ISDT is purely an amateur event, with no prize money awarded to the competitors. Rather, the riders receive simple Olympic-style medals: a gold for a perfect score on the trail, plus requisite bonus points; a silver for less than 50 penalty points; and a bronze for finishing the event. Those small medals are the most cherished objects in the world of off-road motorcycling. To just finish the Six Days' is no mean feat.

Until the early 1960s, most American motorcyclists had not even heard of the ISDT, and few had ridden it. During its era of isolation from 1920 through 1945, the American motorcycle industry, supported by the policies of the AMA, simply regarded the Six Days' as an irrelevant, foreign activity that had nothing to do with motorcycling on this side of the Atlantic. This started to change when a handful of the nation's best offroaders began to take an interest in the event. One of the first was New York BSA rider Tom McDermott, who entered the ISDT in Wales in 1949 and became the first American to win a gold medal. However, such accomplishments remained obscure until *Cycle World* began to report on the involvement of Americans in international competition. In part because he was accessible to the California-based media, Bud Ekins became the Marco Polo of off-road motorcycling. He sallied forth into strange lands and brought back large and exciting tales of the legendary ISDT. He had ridden scrambles in England and motocross in France in the early 1950s, and entered the ISDT in Wales in 1961, where he won a silver medal. This wasn't easy, because the AMA had no affiliation with the International Motorcycling Federation, so American riders had to jump through difficult administrative and diplomatic hoops to participate at the international level. For example, to ride in the 1962 ISDT, John Penton had to obtain his international license through Canada.

John Penton at his first International Six Days Trial; Garmisch-Partenkirchen, West Germany, 1962 (Penton family photo).

John Penton and his long-time friend and teammate, Leroy Winters, in 1964 (Jerry West photo).

John Penton and Bud Ekins at the International Six Days Trial at Garmisch-Partenkirchen, West Germany, 1962 (Penton family photo).

John Penton, going flat out during a special test at the 1969 ISDT at Garmisch-Partenkirchen, West Germany (Jerry West photo).

Penton riders at San Pellegrino, 1968. Left to right, John Penton, Leroy Winters, Tom Penton, and Dave Mungenast (Dave Mungenast photo).

Penton, riding the 250cc BMW at Garmisch-Partenkirchen, was joined by Ekins on a 650cc Triumph, and Alaskan George Streck, Jr., riding a 250cc Greeves. Both Penton and Ekins finished, with Ekins taking a gold, and Penton taking a silver after falling and injuring a knee. Ekins remembers the crash. "John must have been running late, because I had a much later starting number, and I should not have even been near him. But I saw him crash, and that BMW just went end over end. I don't know how it even stayed in one piece, and I don't know how he could get back on and finish."

John Penton has two special memories from his first ISDT. One was a visit by Ekins' good friend Steve McQueen, who was in Germany to film "The Great Escape." In fact, Ekins had taken leave from the movie set as McQueen's stunt double to compete in the Six Days'. It was Ekins—not McQueen—who actually made that famous jump aboard a Triumph. The second thing Penton found memorable was the plethora of small motorcycles entered in the ISDT. His BMW, which was a mid-range enduro bike in the United States, and significantly

John Penton, Dave Mungenast, Leroy Winters, and Bud Green at Garmisch-Partenkirchen in 1969 (Jerry West photo).

smaller than Ekins' big Triumph, was relatively large in the Six Days' setting. John says, "Little motorcycles were zipping by me all the time. They were all over the place. I couldn't believe how fast they went and how well they handled the trail." In fact, the top rider of the event was a German who achieved 599.701 out of a possible 600 points on a 50cc Kreidler. For John, this experience reinforced his beliefs about the viability of lightweight, off-road motorcycles.

John Penton was smitten with the International Six Days' Trial, but was unable to return for the 1963 event in Czechoslovakia. After winning the Corduroy again that year, he had to cancel his trip to Europe when his infant son Tim—the only child in the family belonging to both him and Donna—was stricken with life-threatening encephalitis. Tim recovered, but John's ISDT hiatus continued through 1964 while the family struggled with extraordinary medical bills. However, he returned aboard his BMW in England in 1965—alongside good friend Leroy Winters aboard a Honda— but did not finish. But in Sweden in 1966 Penton earned a bronze medal, riding his BMW for the final time. Having become a regional distributor for Husqvarna in 1967, John entered the Zachopane, Poland ISDT aboard the Swedish brand. It was the first time America fielded a major team, consisting of Bud Ekins, Dave Mungenast, Malcolm Smith, Leroy Winters, John Nelson, and Penton. However, it proved an historic Six Days' in other respects, since it was there that John met people with whom he would collaborate to create the Penton motorcycle. In that respect, Zachopane may have been the most important Six Days' of John's life.

Penton competed in the ISDT three more times. At San Pellegrino, Italy, in 1968, and at Garmisch-Partenkirchen, Germany, in 1969, he was aboard his new Penton motorcycle. This caused a lot of unhappiness with Husqvarna, who had expected John to devote his full talents to their Swedish product. At El Escorial, Spain, in 1970, John rode a Husky, relying on his sons to uphold the good name and reputation of the Penton brand. Today John says with a smile, "I think I could have gotten a gold at El Escorial if I had been riding a Penton."

El Escorial proved to be a special ISDT. It marked the point when John Penton shifted his involvement from competitor to mentor. Subsequent to 1970, John began to take on the ISDT as a patriotic crusade, sponsoring Trophy Teams built around his sons, their cousins, and other young champions chosen from the Penton extended family. El Escorial also made Malcolm Smith an American motorcycling legend and introduced and glorified the ISDT to the whole nation. Jack Penton, who was only 16 at the time, remembers the airplane trip to compete in his first ISDT as a member of the American Silver Vase Team. He recalls, "I was sitting next to a suntanned, blonde guy from California. We started talking, and I learned he was also on his way to El Escorial. It was Bruce Brown, who was then in the final stages of filming *On Any Sunday*." When released, the film contained beautifully moody scenes of Malcolm riding through the mist of a dim and frosty morning, high in the mountains of Spain.

Bud Ekins, Malcolm Smith, the *Cycle World* coverage of the ISDT at Garmisch-Partenkirchen in 1962, Bruce Brown and his ground-breaking motion picture a decade later, and John Penton and his family were all key participants in the off-road revolution that swept American motorcycling. For John especially, the ISDT became a turning point. It is where he confirmed the ideas and met the business partners who helped bring his vision of a better off-road motorcycle to fruition. Today John Penton will smile and run his hand over his scalp in that trademark gesture that means there's something exciting going on inside, and say, "Man, I just can't believe it. I'm just this guy from the East, a guy from Ohio, and I know all these great people in motorcycling—Bud Ekins, Preston Petty, Ted Lapadakis—and these guys from Europe—Erik Trunkenpolz, Arnaldo Farioli, Sante Mazzarolo—and it all happened in Europe. Every year we would meet up at the ISDT and that's where business was done. That's where the contacts were made and business ventures started. Even with the guys from California, it was usually at the ISDT somewhere in Europe when the deals were made."

As for Penton's personal performance, Malcolm Smith says, "I never saw a more determined rider. I think John Penton wanted an ISDT gold medal more than anything else in his life." But it was not to be. In eight outings, John Penton rarely failed to finish the ISDT, but he never earned the coveted gold medal. That task would be left to his sons and their peers who would bring worldwide recognition to both America and the name Penton.

9

Enter the Penton

In addition to becoming the eastern United States Husqvarna distributor in 1967, John also met a Cleveland-based Hungarian importer named Fritz Dengel who was trying to distribute the Hansa motorcycle, manufactured by the Austrian firm, KTM (Kronreif, Trunkenpolz of Mattighofen). The Sachs-powered Hansa was Dengel's brainchild, its name selected to be reminiscent of Honda, which was taking the American market by storm. Dengel wanted Penton Brothers to become dealers for the bike, so John accepted a couple of Hansas and turned them over to his young sons for testing. The prognosis was not favorable; Jack's broke in half the first time he raced it. It was really a small street motorcycle, converted to a not-so-good competition bike, but John found the Sachs engine promising.

John's proposal for a small-displacement off-road bike had been rejected by Husqvarna, so he was looking for opportunities among other manufacturers. At the ISDT in Poland later that year, Penton met Siegfried Stuhlberger, a young rider working for KTM. Stuhlberger, whom John nicknamed Ziggie, was riding a prototype off-road motorcycle with a 50cc Sachs engine. John was captivated by the vehicle, which included elements he thought appropriate for an effective off-road machine. Stuhlberger invited Penton to come to Mattighofen, Austria, after the Six Days' to see the KTM factory and meet its owner, Erik Trunkenpolz.

Partners of the off-road motorcycle revolution; Erik Trunkenpolz and John Penton (Jerry West photo).

Penton pitched Trunkenpolz on his ideas for a small-displacement off-road motorcycle for the American market. Trunkenpolz, who was disenchanted by the poor showing of the Hansa, was skeptical. Finally, Penton told Trunkenpolz he would give KTM $6,000 to build a prototype motorcycle according to his specifications. Having nothing to lose in the deal, Trunkenpolz approved the project.

Penton immediately returned to Europe in October 1967, with Fritz Dengel in tow, and the two met Erik Trunkenpolz and his assistant Kalman Cseh at the annual motorcycle show in Milan, Italy. There they selected the various parts they would need—forks, fenders, fuel tank and sheet metal, controls, and so on—to assemble the prototype, which would feature a Sachs engine and a KTM-built frame. Penton was undertaking the very process he had described to friends five years earlier: picking the best of each major component in order to build a better motorcycle. By December a running prototype was shipped to Amherst for evaluation by John and Ted.

The bike was a rather spindly-looking little machine, clearly carrying no unnecessary weight. It was powered by a 16-horsepower, 125cc Sachs engine with a five-speed gear box.

PENTON SIX·DAY

CHECK THESE SPECS

125cc – 5 Speed – 15½ HP
53" Wheelbase – 185 lbs.
– 10½" Clearance
Sachs Six Days Engine
Full 250 Size Ceriani Forks
2.75 x 21" Motocross Tire
3.50 x 18" Motocross Tire
Ceriani Rear Shocks
Magura Six Day Controls

Available with lighting kits, enduro speedo kits, and mufflers to replace the high-performance exhaust system. Fully guaranteed immediate parts availability. These bikes are in production now and are available for delivery

Penton IMPORTS

1423 FOSTER PARK RD. AMHERST, OHIO 44001 – TEL. (216) 282-6161

The first advertisement for the new Penton brand motorcycle appeared on page 5 of the May 7, 1968 issue of *Cycle News East*. The photo in the ad was of the prototype, not the production model, as revealed by the chrome plated exhaust system (Courtesy of Penton Imports).

The Penton prototype, photographed in December, 1967. The production models did not have a chrome exhaust pipe (Jerry West photo).

It had a 53-inch wheel base and over 10 inches of ground clearance, with a 3.50 x 18 rear wheel and a 2.75 x 21 front. It had Ceriani suspension on both ends, and Magura controls. Its silver frame was complemented nicely by polished aluminum fenders, rolled rib aluminum rims, and the whole package was highlighted by a round, green gas tank with white trim, and yellow racing number plates. It was pleasing to the eye, and Penton intended to bring the bike in for $650 or less, since other European sport motorcycles of similar displacement were available for around $600. Because of the high-quality components used in their construction, the motorcycles were projected to cost John nearly $400 each when placed in mass production.

Arrangements were made to go into production immediately, and the first shipment of ten Pentons arrived in Ohio on March 7th, 1968. By the 8th, six of them were on their way to the Stone Mountain national enduro in Georgia, to be ridden on March 10th by Dave Mungenast, Leroy Winters, Tom Penton, Larry Maiers, Al Born, and John. It was a very gutsy move to take new, untried motorcycles right out of the crate and debut them at an AMA national championship event. It was to be a tough environment, under the scrutiny of the best and most seasoned enduro riders in America. Under the circumstances, the Penton riders did well. Tom Penton was Bantamweight class champion, and Al Born also won his class. Leroy Winters and John Penton placed second and third respectively in the A Lightweight class. John admits, "I don't think anyone was very impressed with the motorcycle at Stone Mountain, but the fact that some top riders were riding them got peoples' attention."

This is the approach the company would adopt in marketing the Penton, putting it in the hands of respected top competitors to be tested under fire in all types of off-road competition. Rod Bush, who worked for Penton Imports and later became the president of KTM USA, says he originally became a Penton dealer because, "This fast kid named Jack Penton kept blowing by us at hare scrambles in Ohio and Pennsylvania. He was coming by on his rear wheel in sections where the rest of us were off and pushing. Some of us figured we could ride more like that if we were riding a Penton." Built around the competitive image of John and his sons, the Penton brand was promoted by emphasizing performance and personality. Advertisements proclaimed Penton victories at prestigious events, and frequently those ads contained a picture of John with persuasive language describing, in his own words, how the Penton motorcycle was built for champions.

From Stone Mountain the Penton crew went on to Daytona, where they entered the new motorcycle in the Alligator enduro, and planned for the motorcycle's commercial debut at the annual Daytona trade show. Leroy Winters prepared the Penton Imports booth by setting up a display that left no doubt the new Penton was a purpose-built off-road motorcycle. Kathie Towne, who helped staff the booth, recalls, "Leroy dragged in a big pile of rocks and set a new Penton on top of it. It really go a lot of attention."

What Penton Imports and KTM had accomplished between September 1967 and the Daytona product debut was almost unthinkable: moving a product as complex as a motor vehicle from an exploratory discussion to a commercially available, serial-production machine in less than six months. Furthermore, the Pentons that first competed at Stone Mountain were not race shop specials, tended by an army of factory engineers. They were available to anyone for $650. In fact, those who rode them at Stone Mountain bought and paid Penton Imports for them. Al Born still proudly displays his bill of sale for Penton #V003, signed by John Penton.

Unlike other companies, Penton Imports did not sponsor riders or pay professionals to fly in, ride an event, then fly home. This would have been contrary to the Penton work ethic and the Penton sense of family. Rather, John Penton gave young riders jobs at Penton Imports where they earned a wage while they learned the Penton way. They learned to set up and maintain their own motorcycles, and, like everyone else on the team, they helped load up the big Penton Cycle Liner and shared the driving task to and from major events all over the nation. Larry Maiers, who became president of Penton

Imports, says, "I had been with Penton only a couple of days, and the Bad Rock Six Day qualifying trial was coming up the next weekend. All the kids loading up the bus said, 'Come on. We're going to Oregon.' I joined up, and it was unbelievable. That thing had about an 800-mile range. It had bunks inside, and we just went like hell. When we stopped for fuel some of the guys would go grab a big sack of burgers, then we were on our way again. Some slept, some drove, and they changed drivers at full speed. We drove from Ohio to Oregon nonstop, did the event, then drove back home and went to work."

The new Penton that appeared at Stone Mountain was not the first shot fired in the off-road motorcycle revolution. As early as 1964, Ducati had introduced its Mountaineer, equipped for trail riding. In 1965 Bultaco introduced the 200cc Matador, a street-legal enduro bike, and in 1966 it advertised its Campera as "the city bike that's at home in the woods." However, most of these early attempts were just modified street models, and others were not robust enough for true competition. The Hodaka Ace 90 appeared in 1964 and became very popular, especially in the western states. It had only four speeds, however, and its little 90cc engine lacked reliability when it was punched out to a larger size or souped up for better performance.

As one might expect of motorcycles with a five-month development life, the Pentons that arrived at Stone Mountain had problems. John and Leroy Winters had a major row when Leroy, frustrated with fouled spark plugs, tried to break open the air box of his Penton, right under the public eye in the Town and Country Motel parking lot in Dalton, Georgia. As with most of John's disputes with friends and colleagues, the disagreement left no permanent damage. Having met Leroy several years earlier at the Jack Pine, John nicknamed him Hilly Billy because of his pronounced Arkansas accent. It was a moniker that Leroy thoroughly enjoyed, and the two remained dear friends until Leroy's death in February, 1999.

The early Penton models also had gear box problems which were not discovered until the bikes were in the field. Texan Richard Sanders, who became the largest Penton dealer in the

The new and improved 1971 Penton, complete with enduro kit (Penton Imports photo).

nation, explains why the Penton was different: "All of the early off-road bikes had their problems. They were designed to be light, and they often broke. But the difference was the guys at Penton, who took a personal interest and got right on it. They cared about their product and their reputation, and they fixed the problems as quickly as they could. Dealers and customers appreciated this, and it's probably why the Penton survived." Bob Bennett, of Mason City, Iowa, who was one of the first Penton dealers and still sells KTM motorcycles, concurs: "The whole Penton family rode their products. They were down-to-earth people you could talk to, and if something went wrong they tried to make it right."

Pennsylvanian Paul Danik, one of the driving forces behind the formation of the Penton Owners Group, purchased his first Penton at the age of 15. It was one of the early bikes and the gear box promptly broke. Danik's dealer, who also was

The Penton line of motorcycles as depicted in a brochure from 1973
(Brochure from the Roy Mauldin collection).

concerned, took Danik and his Penton to Amherst, Ohio, to see John. John and Ted had sorted out the problem, but had not yet had time to send training information and upgraded parts to their dealers. John accepted the Pennsylvania duo and their broken Penton as an opportunity. He disassembled and repaired young Danik's gear box, taking Danik through the process step by step. Then he said, "There! Now I want you to go back and be my man in Pennsylvania to show people how to fix their Pentons." Danik says, "Can you imagine the impression that made on me? Here I was 15 years old, and John Penton personally fixes my gear box, then tells me he's entrusting me to fix other Pentons. I became a fan for life." Danik went on to win an ISDT gold medal aboard a Penton.

Later, Penton introduced a 250cc model, manufactured with improper heat treating in its kickstarter shaft. Shafts were breaking all over the country. Rather than rely on KTM to solve the problem, which could have taken months, Ted Penton machined a big batch of shafts and had them heat treated and

Specs for the Sachs-powered 100cc Berkshire and 125cc Six-Days' models, and the KTM-powered 175cc Jackpiner, introduced in 1972 (Brochure from the Roy Mauldin collection).

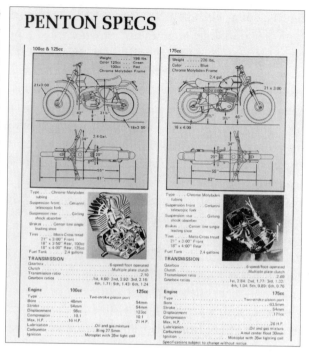

tested locally. Then he hit the road, visiting as many Penton dealers as possible to personally fix the broken bikes. Ted's lifelong friend Norm Miller relates, "One night Ted was replacing the shaft in someone's Penton, and some guy was there spouting off about his Bultaco this and his Bultaco that. He was going on about how a Penton was a piece of crap and his Bultaco had never broken a kickstarter shaft. Ted finally had enough of it and said, 'I'll tell you what, when your Bultaco does break, let's just see if Mr. Bultaco comes around to fix it!' " It was this pride and personal touch by which the Penton survived and became a legendary name in a vigorously competitive market. The Pentons placed their name and staked their reputation on their products. They rode their products in top-level competition, and followed up quickly and conscientiously—and personally, whenever possible—to keep their products running.

Yet this hands-on, fix-it-now attitude did not always endear them to the KTM factory. When Ted and the boys had

figured out a solution to a problem, Ted would machine a prototype part and John would jump on an airplane for Austria. He
would convene a meeting with Erik Trunkenpolz and his engineers. The meeting would begin cordially, as most international meetings do, with smiles and mutual praise and
congratulations all around about the fine business they were
doing together. Then John would introduce his problem and
describe its seriousness. The atmosphere would cool; the Austrians didn't like being told their work was flawed. Then John
would lay out the solution, haul the prototype part out of his
briefcase, and tell the engineers what changes they needed to
make in their manufacturing process.

The Austrians really didn't like this, but it worked. Patricia Penton Leimbach once described the relationship in one of
her columns, "John and his Austrian factory owner rant and
rave and tear their hair in separate languages; they don't
speak for a day, then fall on each other's necks, shake hands,
and part like brothers, business mission accomplished."
Through this process of constantly designing improvements
into the product, Penton ended up with a motorcycle that

Husqvarna-mounted John Penton on his way to a gold medal and an all-out
win at the 1968 Berkshire International Trial in Massachusetts (Boyd
Reynolds, Action Sports photo).

differed significantly from other Sachs-powered motorcycles on the market. While several competitors used the same basic Sachs engine, the Penton power plants were individually stripped down and reassembled at the KTM factory, to be brought up to the specifications dictated by Penton Imports.

Just how quickly the Pentons could make product improvements was demonstrated when the team showed up in Massachusetts at the Berkshire International Trial on May 18th, 1968, just a little over two months after their Stone Mountain debut. The air box that had frustrated Leroy Winters was totally redesigned, and the Penton team, consisting of Tom Penton, Winters, Al Born, and Bud Green, won the manufacturer's championship title. It was the first time Penton Imports had entered a major event with an official manufacturer's team.

Since an off-road motorcycle should carry its rider trouble free through mud and water, the Penton team paid a lot of attention to the air induction system that Leroy Winters had deemed inadequate on the first production model. Air box design improvements came quickly, and by 1969 the frame's main backbone tube was replaced with a ventilated box-shaped section through which air was drawn from under the gas tank, down through a tube into the air box, then into the carburetor. It was called the "high-breather" frame, and in theory and design was similar to the late 1950s NSU street bike that carried John Penton to so many championship enduro victories.

Durability over rough terrain also is essential, resulting in a kind of engineering paradox. Lightness is necessary for performance and good handling, but lightness comes from thinner or smaller tubing, and castings with less bulk. But if parts are too thin and too light, they will break, which was the case with the first production run of Pentons. As frames broke, Penton Imports directed KTM in where to add gussets. When the four-lug rear wheel drive plate proved inadequate, KTM installed a steel band around it as a temporary fix while a new and stronger six-lug plate was designed and produced.

Because the motorcycles were updated as frequently as Penton Imports and KTM considered appropriate, it is somewhat artificial and possibly misleading to identify Pentons in terms of model years. Although significant changes were sometimes introduced on a model-year basis, such as an all-new frame in 1972, improvements and changes frequently appeared at midyear. Identifying the year of a Penton can be tricky business, requiring extensive technical and historical knowledge of the brand. Members of the Penton Owners Group (P.O. Box 756, Amherst, Ohio 44001; www.PentonUSA.org) are expert in these matters, and have produced written guidelines for Penton identification.

The first Pentons to arrive in America were nicely proportioned, but a bit toy-like in appearance, mainly because there was a lot of daylight showing around their small Sachs engine. They just didn't have that packed-with-power look inherent in the big, black engine of a Husqvarna. That changed quickly with the company's policy of constantly upgrading the product. By 1970 the basic Sachs engine had sprouted a huge, square-finned cylinder, designed for as much cooling area as possible, and a big "sunburst" cylinder head that left just enough room between the head and the gas tank to change a spark plug. It had become a serious-looking machine, available in Berkshire (100cc) and Six-Days (125cc) models.

Cycle News described just how far Penton motorcycles had come from the days of makeshift changes in street motorcycles for off-road use: "Everything is right where an experienced rider would put it if he were setting the machine up for an enduro . . . In our opinion, serious enduro riders should be thankful that John Penton got tired of spending endless hours setting up bikes to ride enduros and decided to design a machine ready to ride. Not a compromiser when it comes to woods racing, he has succeeded far better than any of the larger manufacturers."

The Penton had become a front-line warrior in motorcycling's off-road revolution, but something else had happened that John Penton had never reckoned on, as more and more Pentons began to show up at amateur motocross events throughout America. The Penton, it turned out, was suitable for both off-road endurance riding and full-out racing. The company shifted its approach to accommodate both markets, offering their bikes in stripped-down form, with an optional enduro kit available for very little extra cost. The *Cycle News* product test explained, "The bike comes without lights or speedometer. For an additional 45 bucks you get extra handlebars, extra rear sprocket, lights, a special deep water air cleaner cover, and a VDO speedometer. This has to be the buy of the century!" John Penton had not created simply a good off-road motorcycle. He had created an off-road convertible, proficient—with minor modifications—at multiple tasks and different types of competition.

By the time of the laudatory *Cycle News* story, it was not uncommon to see Pentons dominating their engine classes in most national championship enduros, with Bud Green winning the Stone Mountain Enduro outright aboard a Penton in 1970. Having clearly established itself in the American off-road motorcycle market, Penton unveiled an all-new product in September, 1971. As he had done at Stone Mountain three years before, John introduced the bikes in a tough, no-nonsense environment, this time on the Isle of Man, as mounts for the American Trophy Team at the ISDT. Gene Cannady, Tom and Jack Penton, Dane Leimbach, Lars Larsson, and Dick Burleson competed aboard Pentons that were new from the ground up.

Penton riders dominate the Cotton Bowl Enduro at Memphis, Texas, circa 1970. In the center are Jack (overall winner) and Tom Penton. Second from far left is ISDT medalist Mike Lewis (Mike Lewis photo).

The chrome moly frame was totally redesigned and the endearing, little egg-shaped steel gas tank was gone, replaced by a more ergonomic, flat-sided, fiberglass design. Burleson's and Larsson's mounts carried a prototype 175cc KTM-designed engine, scheduled for introduction in serial production machines in 1972. Managed by John, the team earned five gold medals and delivered the best Trophy Team performance ever, finishing fourth in the world.

The personalized approach to business of the Penton family resulted in a world-class motorcycle with a world-class reputation. Yet big changes were on the way for Penton Imports, as the motorcycle evolved toward a product more directly competitive with Husky, and as its manufacturing partner in Austria—now convinced of the viability of its product and the profitability of the American market—became jealous of the name it carried on its gas tank.

Behind the scenes, Penton Imports was dealing with a fundamental conflict of interest. Because he needed to aggressively market two of America's leading off-road brands, John competed personally on Husqvarnas in national enduros, leaving exposure of the Penton brand to his family members and riders like Leroy Winters, Bud Green, and Doug Wilford. Husqvarna, which was directing competition to the Penton by planning to introduce its own 175cc motorcycle in 1972, wanted full control of its lucrative U.S. market. John Penton, who was also planning to introduce larger engines, needed to focus exclusively on the motorcycle that carried his family name. By mutual consent, John and Husqvarna formed a new corporation to take over his eastern U.S. Husky distributorship, effective January 1, 1972. John and Ted were principals in the new organization, eventually selling out their shares to the Swedish parent company in 1974. Simultaneously, Husqvarna negotiated a similar acquisition of Edison Dye's rights in the western United States, making the parent company its own exclusive and comprehensive American distributor.

With his marketing conflict resolved, John Penton moved quickly to reposition his product in the marketplace, announcing in March 1972 that a 175cc Penton was on the way. This was not just another "punched-out" Sachs, because Penton had been collaborating with KTM since 1970 to build an all-new engine. Appearing in May 1972, it was a 26 horsepower, 171cc six-speed power plant designed by Alois Marowetz with the help of Siegfried Stuhlberger, with the letters "KTM" proudly cast into its side covers. Originally designed as a 388cc engine, but introduced as a 175, the new power plant provided room for plenty of growth and development. Jack Lehto, who joined Penton Imports in 1971, rode on the American Silver Vase team at the Isle of Man that year, and became CEO of the reorganized Husqvarna distributorship in 1972, says, "The new engine established KTM's reputation as a major engineering force in the motorcycle industry. John had become very frustrated with KTM because it took so long to develop the engine, but Mr. Trunkenpolz wanted to get it right. And that's what they did. Pound for pound, it was the most powerful two-stroke engine in its class."

The new 175cc Penton was named the Jackpiner, joining its smaller sisters, the 100cc Berkshire and the 125cc Six-Days, both of which still carried the Sachs-based engine. All three were available in motocross and kitted enduro models. Then, at year end, Penton Imports expanded its product line even further, announcing the Penton Trials, an observed trials bike assembled in England by Teddy Wassell. John says, "I made a deal for 50, and he sent me 100. I guess he needed to get rid of some Sachs engines. Boy, we had some words over that." He shakes his head and laughs, "I thought we were never going to sell all those trials bikes. But we weren't the only company in the industry disappointed by the trials market." From the trials bike came the Penton Mud Lark, modified to capture a broader market of casual, non-competitive trail riders.

The new KTM engine gave Penton Imports a whole new platform from which to expand its line and go head-to-head against the traditional big boys, such as Husqvarna and CZ, not to mention the Japanese who were, by 1972, aggressively developing competitive off-road bikes in the larger displacement classes. Working from their new platform, Penton and KTM introduced a 250cc model in 1974, and a 400cc in 1975.

Although Pentons were still known in the United States primarily for their suitability as enduro motorcycles, it was this new engine that powered KTM to a 250cc manufacturer's world championship in the motocross Grand Prix in 1974, ridden by Russian Gennadij Moiseev. The engine also proved strong enough to compete in American dirt-track racing, and in 1976 Penton collaborated with Kenny Roberts to build and sell 250cc short track racers. John says, "Erik Trunkenpolz thought we were crazy to build a short tracker. We didn't build very many, but the few we built gave Penton and the new KTM motor some really high-profile exposure. They really enhanced the reputation of the brand in the American market." Mike Kidd earned a podium finish aboard the KTM short tracker at the Houston Astrodome in 1980.

Following the introduction of the 250cc KTM-powered Penton, *Cycle News* revisited the product in August 1975. It concluded that John's concept of the purpose-built, convertible off-road motorcycle had only improved with age, stating, "Right now there is no other motorcycle available that you can buy off a dealer's floor, and, with the addition or removal of lights, go out and be competitive in a two-day trial, local enduro or motocross, or a national motocross or enduro." Ironically, even after the Penton concept of a multipurpose, convertible off-road motorcycle had proven popular with customers and the media, KTM came out with totally separate motocross and enduro models in 1976, attempting to capitalize upon the Moiseev Grand Prix victories.

There is no telling where John Penton could have taken his motorcycle company, given a level playing field. However, this was not to be the case. As early as 1970, disturbing changes in the global economy and U.S. economic policy began to militate against Penton Imports and other American importers. Ironically, at the very peak of its prestige in the marketplace, the Pentons' business operations came under siege by hostile forces that would prove fatal to the brand, yet leave KTM a strong player in American off-road motorcycling.

10

Penton Imports and
Hi-Point Accessories

In the spring of 1967, John Penton became the official distributor of Husqvarna in the eastern United States. Edison Dye, who had been the sole Husky distributor, was not happy to lose his eastern territory, but with a boom in the popularity of off-road motorcycling, there was plenty of business for both. Furthermore, Dye's passion was motocross and off-road racing; Penton's was enduro and trail riding, so the two provided Husqvarna with a balanced and comprehensive marketing team.

With the arrival of the new Penton motorcycles from Austria in 1968, John Penton became an importer, not just a product distributor. Because there were legal restrictions against importing through the Pentons' licensed retail corporation, John, Ike, and Ted set up Penton Imports, although the firm remained unincorporated until April 30, 1970. By now, Bill was fully involved in running the farm, and did not participate much in the motorcycle businesses. Surprisingly, there was never a contract between Penton Imports and KTM. John Penton and Erik Trunkenpolz did business with a handshake. After John determined that his motorcycle's Stone Mountain debut had been satisfactory, he simply contacted Trunkenpolz and said, "Make us 50 or so more," which KTM undertook on the basis of a bank deposit in Deutschmarks. Penton Imports purchased its first advertisement for Penton motorcycles in

Cycle News East in May 1968, and Ted began setting up dealers throughout the nation.

Because collaboration with KTM frequently took John to Europe, he began to search for other products to sell through his new company. Matt Weisman, whose advertising agency had served the Penton motorcycle dealership, dissolved his company in 1969 and went to work full time for Penton Imports, helping John launch the new Hi-Point brand of motorcycle accessories. One of the first, and one of the most profitable on a long-term basis, was the Hi-Point boot, manufactured in Italy by Alpinestar.

Along with his desire for a better enduro motorcycle, John also believed that riders deserved better, more functional clothing. Lace-up lineman's boots just weren't good enough. One year at the Jack Pine, John sewed his leather pants to the tops of his boots, trying to keep the Michigan sand out of his shoes. Unfortunately, he fell off his bike and into a creek, filling his pants with water like a fisherman's waders. Obviously, not all of John's ideas were good ideas, and this one no doubt convinced him that a better boot was in order.

According to Larry Maiers, the profitable connection between Penton Imports and Alpinestar was the result of a mistake. Penton Imports had already imported a few boots from Europe in the late 1960s, but had made no serious commitments. During one of John's trips to Europe in 1970, he wandered into Alpinestar by accident. Maiers says, "He was lost, and just kind of wandered in, and before he left he had struck up a friendship with Sante Mazzarolo and executed one of his handshake deals to have Alpinestar modify their products for the American off-road motorcycle market." It was a classic John Penton move to turn a mistake into an opportunity. From that serendipitous beginning, Penton Imports went on to nearly control the American off-road riding boot market. Malcolm Smith, who was at the time a competitor of Hi-Point, estimates that in the mid-1970s Penton Imports had an 80 percent share of the boot market. To their successful line of off-road boots, Hi-Point added a line of Alpinestar road racing boots endorsed by Kenny Roberts.

The name "Hi-Point Accessories" came from John Penton's six-year domination of the Canadian national championship at the Corduroy Enduro. "High point" was the term the Canadians used to describe the winner. John and his family undoubtedly heard the term "high point" hundreds of times, so he adopted it as a name for his accessory business. After all, the slogan of Penton motorcycles was, "Built for Champions." It was only fitting that those who rode them should have "high point" riding gear and product enhancements.

Much of the success of Hi-Point Accessories can be attributed to the creative dealing of Larry Maiers. Maiers was born in 1939 in Lansing, Michigan, the home of the Jack Pine Enduro. He recalls it as an exciting annual festival, for weeks after which he and his young friends would tie tool pouches on their bicycles and go crashing about in the woods. As a youth, Maiers met John Penton when he and his Jack Pine crew bunked at his mother's home in Lansing. Maiers owned many motorcycles and had ridden the Jack Pine 13 or 14 times, finishing half the events. Later he worked as a sales representative for Massey-Ferguson, and was given a territory that included Amherst and Lorain County, Ohio. On his travels, he would stop by Penton Brothers and visit with Ted and John. Whether he realized it or not, it was all part of that familiar process of becoming a member of the Penton extended family.

By 1972 the Penton motorcycle had successfully penetrated the American off-road market, and the accessory business was also growing. The Husqvarna distributorship had been turned over to the parent company, which bought some of Penton Imports' assets, hired some of its employees, and leased warehouse space from John, leaving Penton Imports free to focus entirely on its own interests. John approached Larry and asked him to join the team as a vice president and help him achieve better management and control. Maiers took the deal and relocated to Amherst. He quickly learned, however, that regardless of what John said about needing help, he really didn't want much help with the motorcycle business. Maiers says, "I learned pretty quickly that helping John with motorcycles was about like trying to help God save souls. He knew what he was doing and really didn't need much help." Consequently, Maiers focused his efforts on developing a larger and more profitable Hi-Point accessory line, and helping Penton Imports develop its marketing programs and national product distribution system.

Penton Imports was an innovative company. A regional warehouse was set up under J.R. Horne in Amarillo, Texas, in 1968, and Fred Moxley was put in charge of a separate corporation, Penton West, in Sacramento in 1970. As early as 1970, the company rented over-the-road tractors to transport bikes from their port of entry at Baltimore, looking for a way to beat the time and cost of rail travel. When this system was working well, Penton Imports bought two new Kenworth tractors with which they sent bikes west, and brought back produce on the return run. Often one of John's sons or their cousins would drive the rig. In addition to transporting its own inventory, the company became one of the first original equipment distributors to set up its own national dealer shows, and it paid dealers $10 a head per day to send their staff to Penton service schools. These were always held in Amherst, where the dealers could benefit from personal contact with John and Ted, and be immersed in the Penton way of doing things.

One of Penton's advertising and marketing coups was the advent of the Penton Cycle Liners. Through J.R. Horne, John learned that the U.S. Postal Service was liquidating some big custom-built coaches that had been used for a mobile post office experiment in Texas and Oklahoma. They were high quality, 50-foot vans powered by Cummins flat diesels mounted at mid-chassis, built by Crown Coach Corporation of Los Angeles. They were the rough equivalent of what NASCAR drivers now pay $300,000 for, only John picked up three of them for less than $3,000 each. He christened them Penton Cycle Liners, gave them flashy paint jobs, and used them to transport his teams in style and comfort to national championship enduros all over the country. The Penton Cycle Liners brought a touch of class to off-road motorcycling, announcing to the competition that the Penton wrecking crew had arrived. But they were not used just to transport an overdog team. The Cycle Liners were

The mighty Penton Cycle Liner, circa 1972. Riders from left to right are Jack Penton, Tom Clark, Dane Leimbach, Paul Danik, Doug Wilford, Jim Hollander, Jeff Penton, and Bill Uhl (Dave Mungenast photo).

also used as goodwill vehicles, carrying an ample supply of spares and providing support for Penton owners. Jeff Penton recalls, "Sometimes at the end of an enduro, we would just open up the back and give stuff away; tires, and parts, and accessories. It was like a party." The Penton Cycle Liners were time machines, hinting at competitive motorcycling's future, but it would be more than a decade before the Japanese manufacturers began to try to upstage one another with big rigs for their racing teams.

Maiers believes that Hi-Point can be credited with creating the contingency award system that has become a marketing mainstay of the American motorcycle industry. He says, "Bob Hannah, Marty Smith, Brad Lackey, Jimmy Weinert, and others were wearing our boots. Except for Hannah, who did some design and development work for us, all of them were buying their boots retail. That's what riders did in those days. I went to the AMA awards banquet one year and gave each of these guys a fresh pair of boots and a $500 check, and thanked them

Hi-Point accessories were associated with leading champions of the day, such as Bob Hannah and Kenny Roberts. Roberts teamed up with John Penton to market Hi-Point boots, as depicted in this advertisement from 1978 (Courtesy of Penton Imports).

for using our product. That small gesture brought us a heck of a lot of loyalty and goodwill over the years."

Maiers also feels that Penton Imports revolutionized the clothing business by helping it move away from leather as the sole protective material. He says, "The AMA was pretty adamant that protective clothing be made of leather. We were working with suppliers of nylon and other synthetics that we thought were too good to ignore. We went down to Westerville and made a presentation to Bill Boyce. On the strength of that presentation and some testing that Boyce commissioned, the AMA's rules were changed." However, he admits, "Over time we kind of lost out in the clothing business because we didn't catch on to the importance of fashion. Our stuff was enduro based and very functional. The market really took off when some of our competitors started emphasizing color, fashion, and style, and in that department we weren't leading the pack." Dave Duarte, who ran Penton West in 1975, concurs: "I saw the California-based clothing companies coming on with color and style, but the Hi-Point line remained grounded in a conservative enduro market that focused strictly on functionality."

Larry Maiers became president and CEO of both Penton Imports and Hi-Point Accessories. He expanded the Hi-Point line by applying the technique used many times by John: find a manufacturer of a good-quality product and modify it for motorcycle use. For example, John learned that Spectro Oil Co. was experimenting with synthetic lubricants. He field tested their products and was satisfied enough to launch a Hi-Point label two-stroke oil, supplied and packaged by Spectro.

The line also included upgraded racing ignition systems provided by Spanish Motoplat, alloy rims by Sun, air filters by Twin Air, lightweight nylon enduro jackets and pants, knobby tires made by Carlisle and Metzeler, chrome moly handlebars, Lectron carburetors, gloves, goggles, and chest protectors.

Penton Imports and Hi-Point Accessories had a significant impact on segments of the motorcycle industry, both in America and Europe. Alpinestar benefitted enormously from a boot market virtually created by Penton Imports, and other well-known companies might not have survived without the influence of John Penton. Jack Lehto states, "Metzeler might not be here today if it were not for John Penton. They had already lost their automotive market, and were on the way out in motorcycling. Basically, they were making conveyor belts and other industrial rubber products when John Penton decided he wanted Metzeler as OEM tires on Penton motorcycles. This account, and Penton Imports' selection of Metzelers as replacement tires kept Metzeler alive in the motorcycle industry."

John Penton was not content to provide motorcycles, the products you put in and on them, and the clothing for those who ride them. He also found a market in how to transport

Son of Cycle Liner: KTM's big Y2K Kenworth motocross team transporter.

them, and began in 1984 to manufacture high-quality, fiber-glass, enclosed trailers under the Hi-Point brand name. They earned a prestigious reputation, and were a popular product until the recession began to cut into the buyer's ability to pay premium prices when less expensive options were available. Even after the domestic market began to decline, Hi-Point trailers were ordered by well-funded customers in Europe and South America.

Although the Penton brand disappeared from the gas tank of KTM-made motorcycles in 1978, Penton Imports remains a viable company today. Penton Central was closed in 1982 and the Hi-Point Accessories business was sold to Malcolm Smith in 1987, then subsequently to Tucker Rocky three years later. The trailer manufacturing operation was sold to a Lorain-based boat manufacturer in 1998. Penton Imports still distributes German-made PVL high performance racing ignition systems, and provides service for both PVL and Motoplat systems. One of its high-profile customers is the Harley-Davidson race shop, using PVL electronics in the development of the VR1000 Superbike road racer. Today PVL Electronics, a division of Penton Imports, is managed by John's nephew Dane Leimbach.

11

Penton and Motocross

By 1968 John Penton had achieved what he had set out to do a decade earlier when he won the Jack Pine aboard a modified 175cc street motorcycle. He had created a small-displacement motorcycle expressly designed for off-road competition, and its acceptance had been remarkable. Less than twelve months after his initial meeting with Erik Trunkenpolz, more than 35 Penton motorcycles were entered in the 1968 ISDT by both American and European competitors. A motorcycle that had not existed a year prior now represented more than 10 percent of the field at the world's toughest off-road enduro. By the mid-1970s, fully half of the Americans who entered the ISDT were riding Pentons. But American tastes in off-road motorcycling were continuing to change, and through the emergence and popularity of motocross, John Penton found a larger market than he had dreamed of in his quest for a better enduro machine.

"Scrambling," a term used also in Great Britain, had been a popular form of competition in America since the end of the second world war. In scrambles, riders compete on a course laid out over natural terrain, containing both right and left turns, and changes in elevation. Usually these courses were relatively smooth, suitable for the heavy, powerful, four-stroke motorcycles popular in the United States during the 1950s. In Europe, the scrambles courses were usually rougher, better suited for lighter motorcycles with longer suspension and quicker acceleration. Motocross, run on these rough courses, made physical fitness and rider endurance prerequisites for winning. Whereas scrambles were run for a pre-determined number of laps, rarely lasting more than eight to ten minutes, motocross races were based on two 40-minute "motos." They combined endurance with flat-out speed.

The first Americans to witness motocross races were simply astonished. They did not believe it was possible for human beings to ride so hard and so fast for such a long period of time. It was a spectacularly vigorous style of riding, punctuated by wheelies, leaps through the air, and wheel-spinning, dirt-spurting slides through the turns. The Europeans who had conditioned themselves for world championship competition were in such good shape, they invariably rode faster at the end of a moto than at the beginning. A growing interest in this continental form of competition was just one more example of the changing tastes in American motorcycling. Through the broader coverage offered by *Cycle World* and *Cycle News,* which glamorized the international aspects of motorcycling, young Americans began to take an interest in motocross racing, just as they had with the ISDT.

Edison Dye, who was the official American distributor for Husqvarna, realized that motocross, which played before crowds of 30,000 or more people in Europe, was the optimum way to expose his product in its best working environment. However, at that time only the European riders were qualified to present motocross as it was intended. Dye hired Swedish rider Lars Larsson to come to America to help sell Husqvarnas. Lars says, "We took a van with two bikes around to local races. Because I held an FIM international license and was not supposed to be racing in local events, Edison always signed me up as Larry Lawson from San Diego. We would just beat the pants off the local amateur riders, and people would come around after the race to learn more about Husqvarnas. Here I was, supposed to be a Californian, and I could speak almost no English. No matter what they asked me, I'd just smile and say, 'Ya, Ya. Is good Sveedish technology. Is good Sveedish motorcycle.' " This gimmick worked so well that Dye decided to take it to a higher level by creating the Inter-Am motocross series. Hiring

ten top European champions after the close of the Grand Prix
season, he organized an autumn series of races that began in
Massachusetts and crossed the country to California over a
two-month period. Dye had showcased the European stars in
one-off events in California since 1966, and there was a pent-
up demand to see them in other parts of the nation. To his
credit, Dye made his road show something more than a self-
serving Husqvarna benefit. He also hired the factory riders
from CZ, Maico, and Greeves, probably realizing that a rising
tide raises all ships.

What Dye created was not so much a tide as a tidal wave.
With *Cycle News*—now with two editions—carrying timely
information and advertising about the events, the Inter-Am
created a big buzz throughout the motorcycling community,
attracting paying customers in numbers that had not been
seen since the big board track races of motorcycling's pre-1920
glory days. With the international features held on Sunday,
Dye scheduled races for American riders on Saturday, dangling
the carrot that the best would qualify to race against the Europeans. These races drew hundreds of riders, hoping to try their
hands at motocross and—with some luck—test their skills
against the world champions. Dye offered motocross riding
clinics, taught by the likes of world champions Torsten
Hallman and Dave Bickers. The events became great, joyous
festivals, unlike any other event in American motorcycling.
They attracted a largely youthful audience, not unlike the cele-
brants at Woodstock. Motocross, Americans decided, was good
rock and roll.

Edison Dye's Inter-Am started a trend that forever
changed the American motorcycle market, turning young people from traditional American forms of competition—oval
track racing and hill climbing—to European-style motocross.
Motocross caught on so quickly that, by 1970, Penton Imports
shifted its marketing strategy to offer its 100cc and 125cc
Pentons as motocross racers, with an optional kit for those who
wanted enduro bikes. It became common to see "PEN PEN
PEN" listed again and again in the results pages of *Cycle News*.
Moto Beta, Sachs, Hodaka, and other European and Japanese

brands also benefitted from a rapidly expanding motocross market.

That year Charles Dillen, from Belgium—the nation that produced motocross supermen Joel Robert and Roger Decoster—visited America on behalf of the FIM. While observing a routine AMA-sanctioned amateur race at Mansfield, Ohio, he said, "One day you Americans will utterly dominate world motocross." It was an unbelievable statement, and the Americans with him challenged his judgment, stating, "We'll never be able to ride like the Europeans." Dillen waved his arm over the track and calmly responded, "Just look at this. It's just a matter of time and numbers. Belgium is smaller than Ohio, and we have produced world champions. There are hundreds of young people riding here today, and you have hundreds of tracks like this all over a big, big country. Statistically, we Europeans simply don't stand a chance. You have the world's biggest training ground for motocross. The future belongs to you Americans." Eleven years later the American team of Chuck Sun, Johnny O'Mara, Danny Laporte, and Donnie Hansen— then regarded apprentice professionals in America—thrashed their European competitors at the Motocross des Nations, setting off an uninterrupted, thirteen-year American winning streak. Charles Dillen had accurately envisioned the future.

John Penton, both through his motorcycle and his person, was part of the process through which Charles Dillen's prediction came true. Countless young people, including Danny LaPorte and Donnie Emler, developed their skills aboard 100 and 125cc Pentons, and Bob Hannah, Marty Smith, Brad Lackey, and Jimmy Weinert were just a few of the champions whose careers were enhanced through support from Hi-Point products. Yet John Penton's greatest contribution may have taken place at the political level, an arena he usually tries to avoid.

To pull off his rapid-fire, transcontinental road show, Edison Dye partnered with promoters and race track owners across the nation. In 1968 his promoter for the Mid-States International Championship was John Penton and the Amherst Meadowlarks Motorcycle Club, using a race track at New

Philadelphia, Ohio. The weekend followed the usual format: national races on Saturday, qualifying riders for the Inter-Am field on Sunday. The Saturday races were AMA sanctioned. The Sunday races were not, due to a long-term political standoff between the AMA and the FIM. The weekend was a huge success, receiving enthusiastic praise from the fans and the media.

Shortly thereafter, the AMA invoked an old rule that prohibited its members from participating in unsanctioned events. Dick Mann and John Penton were singled out for punishment. Mann's professional license was suspended for the remainder of the 1968 season, a punishment he brushed aside since he had no intention to race again that year. Penton's membership was suspended for six months for his involvement as promoter of the event, and the charter of the Amherst Meadowlarks was revoked. John took his suspension seriously and vowed to fight, it. He intended to ride enduros throughout the winter, including the national championships scheduled during the first quarter of 1969.

The AMA could not have chosen two worse people to pick on. While the Association had been sanctioning amateur motocross races for some years, it had no professional motocross program, and only a few months before had asked both Penton and Mann to serve on a committee to develop such a program. Their treatment was a sorry reward for their leadership in the field.

Furthermore, both men had received the AMA's Most Popular Male Rider award in years past. John Penton was regarded by the motorcycling public as a great competitor and a visionary for his role in bringing the Inter-Am to America. Dick Mann was enormously popular for having taken on the youthful European supermen at New Philadelphia, emerging as top American rider in the process. Their fans were outraged. *Cycle News* published frank but polite editorials urging the AMA to reconsider its autocratic attitude. Its readers were less restrained, sending in letters to the editor expressing indignation and outrage. Some opportunists grasped the moment to create or promote their own splinter organizations.

Besides the fundamental autocracy of its action, the AMA was criticized for inconsistency, since Mann and Penton were not the only ones to participate in unsanctioned events. The AMA countered this criticism foolishly by leveling other suspensions. The Intersport Motorcycle Club, promoter of an Inter-Am in Massachusetts, had its charter revoked; and Joe Bolger, a top New England professional rider, had his license suspended. Shortly thereafter the AMA suspended Gordon Jennings and Jess Thomas for fifteen days for entering an unsanctioned road race. Jennings and Thomas were both editors for *Cycle Magazine,* which had, at that time, the largest circulation in the industry. Apparently no one had reminded AMA Executive Director William Berry that it is unwise to mess with people who buy their ink in 55-gallon drums.

Faced with popular outrage and threats of defection from members and organizations throughout the nation, the AMA Executive Committee rescinded the suspensions by January 1969, and directed Berry to form a committee to reevaluate the rules that prohibited participation in unsanctioned events.

Back in good standing with the AMA, John Penton went about his business to become the 1969 AMA Grand National Enduro Champion, putting an end to Bill Baird's seven years of domination. It was John Penton's best year since 1958 on the AMA enduro circuit, and despite his many individual championship victories over a long career, it was the only year that Penton won the overall championship.

Progressing from the crisis created by the AMA in October 1968, 1969 became a watershed year for the organization. That autumn the AMA Congress, newly created in late 1968, abolished many of its more authoritarian and unpopular rules. Chuck Clayton wrote an editorial heaping praise on the AMA for its forward thinking and willingness to change. Furthermore, Bill Berry used the occasion to announce that the Association had found a way to set aside its differences with the FIM. By breaking its long-standing isolationist traditions, the AMA embarked on a course that would ultimately help Americans dominate almost every area of international competition.

John Penton gives Edison Dye credit for revolutionizing American motorcycle racing. He says, "Edison Dye sold motocross to America." However, John Penton not only provided many of the motorcycles through which a new generation of Americans honed their skills in motocross, he also became—albeit unwillingly—the lightning rod of a storm that blew the American Motorcyclist Association into an exciting new era of growth, expansion, and world prominence.

12

The Third Generation

John Penton is a Promethean personality. He doubts conventional wisdom and defies the established order. He is the bringer of fire, a man whose heat touches everyone around him, leaving inalterable change in his path. But John Penton knows where credit is due. In October, 1988, he was asked by a local reporter to comment on how he had achieved success. Within his response he stated, "People are the name of the game." John knows that the enormous influence he had on motorcycling throughout the world would never have come without the support, energy, dedication, and loyalty of those around him. Central among these is the third generation of the Amherst Pentons, the sons and daughters of the sons and daughters of Harold Penton, John's children, the children in his blended family, and the children of his brothers and sisters.

There was never a time when John Penton's children—whether they were Pentons or Hochenedels—were not around motorcycles. Tom Penton was born the same year that the Penton Brothers opened their motorcycle dealership. Two years later came Jeff, then Jack two years thereafter. These three became key figures in the growth of Penton Imports and, along with their cousins Dane and Ted Leimbach, were the core of some of America's best international enduro teams. All became proficient at scrambles and motocross at an early age, and each entered national championship enduros as soon as they were legally eligible. Jack says, "Actually, I entered a national when I was fourteen, and I helped drive the van on the way home, before I was licensed to drive. We weren't trying to break the law, we just all pitched in on everything, and it seemed like a normal thing to do." Jeff adds, "Same with tractors. We just grew up with them, and it is hard to remember a time when we weren't around motorcycles, or operating trucks or equipment around the farm." Dane comments, "Right, nobody ever taught us how to ride. We just did it. We had a lot of land and woods around our farm, and every spare minute I wasn't doing chores, I was riding my motorcycle." Jeff adds, "When we were little, Dad would ride us around on the roads in the cemetery next to the farm. We would sit in front of him and he would let us work the controls. So, by the time we had a chance to get our own motorcycles, we already knew a lot about how to ride."

A fourth Penton brother, Tim—born seven years after Jack and too late to experience the off-road motorcycling revolution—also became an accomplished rider, but moved in a different direction from his brothers. He graduated at the top of his class at Ohio State, and is today the comptroller for one of the largest school districts in Ohio. Two other cousins, Chris and Mike Kovach, were also involved in motorcycling. Chris and Jack traveled to hare scrambles together, and Chris worked for a period of time at Penton Imports in the service department and driving trucks.

Tom and Jeff got their first motorcycle—a shared gift—at Christmas, 1964. It was a 200cc street Yamaha, not the most suitable bike on which to become off-road champions. Jeff says, "We didn't care what it was. We just took it out and rode it. We rode all through the family's apple orchard, and we learned a way to go cross country, all the way to Dane's house in Vermilion, which was ten miles away." He adds, "Jack didn't have a motorcycle yet, and he was my pusher. He was always on the back of the motorcycle, and when I got stuck, it was Jack's job to hop off and push. Since it had smooth street tires, we were always getting stuck."

Jack thought being the pusher was a lot of fun, but it didn't substitute for having his own motorcycle. John had an old trade-in, step-through Honda that he hung up in the air as part of the sign for the motorcycle dealership. Jack and his sister Laura thought that was poor use of a perfectly good motorcycle, and they nagged John to take it down and give it to them. Finally he did, figuring their messing with it would stop their complaining for at least a few weeks. The kids put gas, oil, and a battery in it, hit the starter, and it fired right up. Ironically, giving the derelict step-through to Jack and Laura probably resulted in more motorcycle sales than using it as a sign. John says, "I was just amazed. The damn thing hung out in the weather for almost a year, and it fired right up and ran just fine. Man, I really used that story to sell a lot of Hondas. I told all of my customers about it; about how tough and reliable Hondas are." Later Jack and Laura stripped it, rebuilt it, and, showing a flair of creativity, painted it purple.

Jeff was the most adventuresome of the brothers. When John was out of town, Jeff would recruit Jack to help him take John's BMW enduro bike for joy rides. Jack says, "Jeff was the only one of us who could start it. I would help hold the bike so Jeff would not tip it over, and he would climb up and get both feet on the starter pedal and just jump and jump and jump until it fired up. Then he would take off and roar around the countryside. There was a hill by the machine shop where he could jump the thing, actually getting both wheels off the ground." Jeff adds, "I heard Dad bragging about how well the front suspension worked when he raced across the ties down the middle of a railroad track at some enduro he had just returned from, so I sneaked the bike out and tried it. I rode it down the middle of a railroad line just as fast as I could." On another occasion Jeff and Jack took John's enduro Husqvarna out and raced it all over the farm. Jack says, "We brought it back dirty. Dad had to know what was going on, but he never said anything to us." Perhaps John judged his sons' behavior in light of his own youthful antics, having more than once "borrowed" his brother Ike's Harley to try to pick up girls.

Tom Penton recalls that his first competition motorcycle was a Suzuki Bearcat, which he rode at his first Jack Pine Enduro at the age of 16. All three of the brothers began their competition careers aboard 73cc Sachs Boondockers and 125cc

CZs, riding at the scrambles tracks throughout northern Ohio. Tom, who favored the small-bore classes and usually rode the 100cc Penton through most of his career, remembers the little Boondocker as one of his favorite motorcycles. About the CZs Jack says, "They weren't like the bikes that Joel Robert and Roger DeCoster made famous. These were clunky little bikes, kind of modified CZ street motorcycles. They even had that funny shifter which flipped over backwards to become the kickstarter."

Tom was 18, Jeff was 16, and Jack was 14 when the Penton motorcycle came on the scene. Already proficient competitors, they used their skills to advance the reputation of the motorcycle. Though they could usually beat the local competition on any reasonably competitive bike, now they were on motorcycles bearing their name, and that got a lot of attention. Many young racers decided they needed to have a Penton motorcycle after they found themselves bested by one of the Penton boys. Within a year the Penton boys took their act international,

Tom, Jeff, and Jack in El Escorial, Spain, 1970 (Jerry West photo).

with Tom riding the ISDT in Italy in 1969, and Jack and Jeff joining the team in Spain in 1970.

Although Jeff rode in only three ISDTs in his brief career, Jack maintains he was the best rider among them. Jack says, "We all had different riding styles, but none of us rode like Dad. Dad was brutal. He just mowed down whatever was in his path. Tom was much more conservative. He was a thoughtful, calculating competitor. People have always told me I was very quick. But I think Jeff embodied all of the qualities. He was fast and aggressive, but always thinking. He was definitely the best in the family." Cousins Dane and Ted Leimbach were also first-class riders. When pressed into service as a Trophy Team alternate at the Isle of Man in 1971, Dane proved to be one of the best riders on the team, winning a gold medal.

Although the Penton and Leimbach boys contributed heavily to Penton's "Built for Champions" motto, winning races was not their only contribution to the family operation. Each, in his own way, contributed to the business of Penton Imports. Jeff worked as a development rider, helped set up service operations at Penton Central in Amarillo, Texas, and later worked in the Hi-Point trailer business. Jack started out setting up new motorcycles at the dealership. Following the demise of the Penton brand, he and Dane worked as consultants to Kawasaki from 1979 to 1981, helping develop their off-road products. Later Jack returned to KTM USA, where he works today as a marketing executive. Tom may have been their best product development man. Jack says, "Tom was always the one with the problem-solving ideas. He didn't even talk to us about it. He would just go off and design a new part and show up at the next enduro with it installed on his bike. We often made fun of him because his stuff was so cobby looking, but it always worked. After Tom made something that solved a problem, Uncle Ted would do his machine shop magic and turn it into something really beautiful that could be put into production." Tom, for example, was the man who developed the folding shift lever that became a standard feature of Penton motorcycles, and was later patented by Yamaha. Dane also became a good machinist under uncle Ted's tutelage. Always a quick learner who could master any mechanical skill, Dane now runs PVL Electronics, a division of Penton Imports.

It is possible that the only glue that held Penton Imports together as a going concern was family. It was not a company with a layered chain of command, policy manuals, job descriptions, or planning procedures. Jack says, "Dad never had a plan for anything, but he had a vision. He knew exactly where he wanted to go, and when he got an idea or a project in his teeth, he bit into it like a bulldog. You weren't invited to go along with it. You were *expected* to, and you really had to be immersed in the Penton culture to understand how you were supposed to make a contribution. He expected us to understand where we fit in and what we were supposed to do next."

It is this family bond that made the Penton competitive at the ISDT. In the 1960s and 70s the ISDT was very different from what it has become today. The best teams and the perennial winners were those who functioned with strict discipline, and whose members were as talented as mechanics as they were as riders. The best teams were the West Germans, the East Germans, and the Czechoslovakians. The two Germanies came by discipline through cultural evolution and an overweening Cold War desire to beat each other. The Czechs achieved excellence through militarism, literally. Prior to 1989, when the communist system began to collapse, their international motorsports programs were managed by the Czech army, and their riders were full-time soldiers, assigned to ride motorcycles. They slept in dormitories, constantly trained at riding and repairing their machines, and lived together. They achieved star-quality results, yet no individual was a star. They were each part of a highly efficient machine in which each member did his part, and understood what the other was thinking.

The Penton family probably came as close as any Americans ever have or ever will to achieving a requisite world-class level of ISDT group mentality and team efficiency. In a way, they achieved it just like the Czechs, although their circumstances were different. The core members of the team worked together, lived together, ate together, and were, in fact, raised together. They knew what each other was thinking, and they understood that individual achievement was subordinate to team results. Furthermore, they had a company commander whose name was John Penton.

If such a description makes the third generation of Amherst Pentons sound like Stepford sons or cookie-cutter automatons, nothing could be further from the truth. All are bright and individualistic, with very different personalities. Family members often comment on the uncanny similarities between the second and third generations of the Penton brothers. Donna Penton says, "Jack is a lot like Uncle Bill, the negotiator. Bill could persuade John to see things a certain way when he wouldn't listen to anyone else in the family. That job has gone to Jack, and he is good at it." Dane comments, "Tom is so much like Uncle Ike. He is a quiet man and an introvert. He would rather just quietly step aside than get wrapped up in some big, noisy conflict. That's how Tom has handled difficult family situations." Jack says, "You know what Uncle Ted was like? Jeff is Uncle Ted all over again. If one of us kids was going to get into trouble, it would be Jeff. He's every bit as stubborn as Dad, and wasn't afraid to stand up to him." So perhaps the fourth brother, Tim, can rightfully be compared to Uncle Hank, who chose to go in a different direction, becoming the Penton whose name rarely appears in connection with motorcycling.

Collectively, the members of the third generation provided the talent and energy that made Penton a household word among motorcycling families throughout the world. But the name Penton was built on more than just kin. John's ability to motivate and inspire loyalty created a vast extended family, many of whom remain dedicated today to the Penton marque. Jack says, "When we start giving credit for what the Pentons accomplished, we should not forget the incredible dealer network that helped make a success of the Penton brand. John and Ted's personal touch in choosing and supporting dealers and their customers created strong and lasting relationships. Our dealers expected a lot from Penton Imports, and they were willing to give a lot in return. They are what took Penton and

KTM through the hard times, and many remain KTM's strongest dealers today."

Creativity ran through the Penton Imports staff. Matt Weisman was one of the best on the team at building workable and effective marketing and public relations programs around John Penton's ideas. In addition to handling the creative process for all advertising and printed material, Weisman worked out a carefully integrated program of awards and recognition for Penton dealers and owners. "Penton Class Winner" stickers were sent to young riders who won races on Pentons, and many pages of each issue of *Keeping Track,* the company newsletter, were devoted to recognizing the achievements of Penton riders, from unknown amateurs to international champions. *Keeping Track* and other recognition programs developed by Weisman made countless young people feel good about themselves and about riding Pentons. When dealers had an idea that sold motorcycles or promoted the marque, *Keeping Track* laid on praise and gave credit where credit was due. Rarely do original equipment manufacturers achieve the kind of positive relationship that existed between Penton Imports, its dealers, and their customers. All were made to feel like members of the Penton family.

John had the vision, and John brought the fire, but John knew it was the power of other people—family, extended family, dealers, and customers—who brought success and turned his visions into reality.

13

ISDT: The Crucible

"Built for Champions" was not some ad copy writer's hollow phrase. The first time a Penton motorcycle turned a wheel was in AMA national championship competition, and during its inaugural season it won prestigious team championship titles at both the Berkshire International Trial and the Canadian national championship Corduroy Enduro. However, it was the International Six Days' Trial that became the crucible for marketing and developing Penton motorcycles, the proving ground to confirm their worthiness for world-class championship competitors.

Less than a year after the assembly of a Penton prototype, the motorcycle made its international debut at the Six Days' at San Pellegrino, Italy. It was one of the most difficult ISDTs in recent memory, the event at which John Penton claimed that each individual day was more difficult than the entirety of the Jack Pine Enduro. Among the 17 Americans entered in the event, 11 were riding Pentons. Furthermore, Penton Imports sponsored a Silver Vase team consisting of Tom Penton, Dave Mungenast, Wolf Jackson, and John Penton. John, living up to his iron man reputation, had ridden the Jack Pine on September 21st and 22nd, broken his collar bone, and departed for Italy on the 23rd. Three members of the team finished the event, placing 10th in world competition. John and Dave both earned bronze medals, and Tom, riding his first ISDT at age 18, earned a silver medal. They were the only Americans to finish the event, so it was an auspicious debut for the marque under trying circumstances.

The ISDT at Garmisch-Partenkirchen, Germany, in 1969 was an easier event. Twenty-three Americans entered and 17 finished. The Penton had a big presence among European competitors, as well as Americans. About the brand's involvement, *Cycle News* reported, "Though the Penton motorcycle is not an American manufactured machine, its design and development by American riders has turned it into a major world competitor in two short years. Many foreign riders entered on Pentons, and many of the machines listed in the results under the KTM brand actually were Pentons, bearing name and all. Altogether, 27 Pentons were entered, and among them were seven gold and nine silver medal winners." Among these were Leroy Winters, Ron Bohn, Dave Mungenast, Ed Schmidt, and John Penton winning silver; Bud Green took a bronze.

The Penton motorcycle and John Penton's commitment to the ISDT significantly improved the position and prestige of America in international competition, a fact that did not go unnoticed in Europe. *Das Motorrad* wrote, "The participation of riders from the U.S. is no longer a game or a joke. They are coming!"

At El Escorial, Spain, in 1970 John changed to a Husqvarna, riding on the American Trophy Team. Husky had not been happy with his appearance aboard a Penton in Garmisch-Partenkirchen and San Pellegrino, since he was head of their eastern U.S. distributorship. But the best-performing American team was the Penton-mounted Silver Vase Team. It was pure Penton Imports, consisting of Tom, Jeff, Jack, and Doug Wilford. Tom and Jeff both earned gold medals; Jack, riding his first ISDT, and Doug earned silver. Jack and Jeff recall their naivete and lack of preparedness in Spain. Jeff says, "There was a tremendous altitude change. We had never experienced anything like that. The day would start off just fine, then we would ride into the mountains where it became very cold. There was actually snow in the mountains. We didn't have any cold weather riding gear, and we about froze." Jack laughs, "Mr. Trunkenpolz loaned Jeff his dressy top coat. There was

The first Penton-sponsored ISDT Trophy Team at the Isle of Man, 1971. Left to right: John Penton, team manager; Gene Cannaday, Tom Penton, Jack Penton, Dane Leimbach, Lars Larsson, and Dick Burleson.

Jeff, riding through the mountains in a man's long coat." El Escorial was John's final ISDT ride.

In 1971 a whole new Penton showed up at the Isle of Man ISDT, sporting a chrome moly frame and a prototype of the new KTM engine that was scheduled for production the following year. The American Trophy Team, which placed fourth, was Penton mounted, consisting of Jack, Tom, Dane Leimbach, Gene Cannady, Lars Larsson, and Dick Burleson. Jeff, who was slated to ride on the team, broke his foot at the Corduroy just days prior, giving Dane his big chance. With 32 Americans entered, 20 finished; all earned gold or silver. Penton riders earning gold consisted of Jack and Tom, Cannady, Leimbach, Larson, Dave Mungenast, and Charles Vincent. Penton rider Mike Lewis earned a silver. Tom, who had taken leave from the Air Force to ride the event, proudly wore his U.S. Air Force insignia on his team uniform.

At Czechoslovakia in 1972, the U.S. Trophy Team consisted of Jeff, Jack, Dane Leimbach, Dick Burleson, Carl Cranke, and Bill Uhl. Again, Dane came in as the alternate, because Tom, who was on military duty in Thailand, could not get leave to ride. He says, "That really upset me. I felt like going AWOL." Jack adds, "I think there was politics and national security involved. I don't think they wanted Tom riding in a communist country while he was still in the U.S. military."

The Penton-mounted Trophy Team receives the ISDT Watling Trophy at Spindleruv Mlyn, Czechoslovakia in 1972. Left to right are Doug Wilford, team manager; Bill Uhl, Dane Leimbach, Jack Penton, Jeff Penton, Carl Cranke, and Dick Burleson (Jerry West photo).

It was a tough event, and a heartbreaker for the Penton team. Dick broke a chain and Jack fouled five spark plugs on the sixth day, losing his gold. All other members of the Trophy Team, plus Penton-mounted Gene Cannady, earned gold medals. Jack earned a silver and Dick finished to get a bronze. With an outstanding performance that turned to a catastrophe in the final hours of the event, the U.S. Trophy Team was given the Watling Trophy, awarded annually in recognition of best effort or most improvement. Out of 32 Americans entered, there were nine gold, three silver, and one bronze medalist. Penton riders represented more than half of the Americans winning gold medals.

With five years of creditable ISDT performance behind it, and two as America's Trophy Team, the Penton motorcycle had earned respect among off-road riders throughout the world, and made America an ISDT contender. Tod Rafferty, in a story after the Czechoslovakian event for *Cycle News,* stated, "Praise to John Penton for coming closer than anyone has in fielding a team potentially capable of challenging the Europeans. And, more important, for not accepting the challenge on their terms. Penton is not into buying high-priced riders, or equipping them with exotic machinery tailored to win one particular event. He has assembled (and, in some cases, sired) a group of young, enthusiastic riders to face off with the big guys. And in two years the upstarts have given the big guys something to think about."

In 1973 the ISDT came to Dalton, Massachusetts. It was America's finest hour for off-road motorcycle competition. The event was built up through a lot of local publicity, and schools in the area closed so children could experience the excitement. Hundreds stood by the roadside and waved little American flags, cheering on each rider, no matter what his nationality. The AMA published a program containing a page explaining the color-coded helmets of the international riders. Citizens stood in front of their homes, program in hand, pointing at the riders as they rushed by and identifying each by the country from which he had come.

Again, Penton Imports fielded the American Trophy Team, consisting of Jack, Jeff, Tom, Dane, Bill Uhl, and Carl Cranke. All earned gold except Tom, who earned a silver, and Jeff, who earned a bronze. Doug Wilford, Joe Barker, and Paul Danik also earned gold medals riding Pentons. The American Six Days' clearly demonstrated to what extent John Penton's motorcycle had become the endurance tool of choice. Forty-five riders out of 300 entries, far more than any other single brand, were riding Penton-designed motorcycles. However, more than 30 of them were labeled KTM, not Penton. Twenty riders took home gold medals riding Penton/KTM motorcycles. Ironically, though the first U.S. ISDT was America's finest hour in Six Days' competition, Husqvarna took the honors, with the team of Ed Schmidt, Ron Bohn, Malcolm Smith, and Dick Burleson winning the Silver Vase. All except Smith had done their ISDT apprenticeships aboard Penton motorcycles.

The American ISDT is still a horror in Jeff Penton's memory. Silicone sealer sloughed off from the inside of his air box, entered the carburetor and affected engine performance, dropping him to a bronze on the third day. Jeff says, "I still think of myself as the guy who let America down. The ISDT in Dalton was our year to win. We were ready for it, and we knew how to ride those Massachusetts woods; I had won the Berkshire. When I dropped to a bronze on the third day, it wrecked the whole team. After that, everyone was just going through the motions, because it was all over." For Jeff, it truly was, because he ended his competitive riding career following the 1973 ISDT. Though the other team members don't believe Jeff should take personal ownership for the defeat, they are also bitter about the ill-fated event. Dane says, "If we were running under today's rules, where you can earn back points and do about anything to your motorcycle, Jeff would have easily gotten back on gold, and we could have won. But that's not how it was back then. When you went down, you went out."

At Camerino, Italy, in 1974, the American Trophy Team included Tom, Jack, Dane, Carl, Joe Barker, and Paul Danik, riding for Penton. Tom, Jack, and Carl earned gold medals. Joe and Paul earned silver, and Dane took a bronze. Both the Penton-mounted U.S. Trophy Team and the Husky-mounted Silver Vase Team earned fourth place.

Returning to the Isle of Man in 1975, the Penton-sponsored Trophy Team consisted of Tom, Jack, Carl, Dane, Eric Jensen,

The Penton Trophy Team at Camerino, Italy, 1974. Left to right: Joe Barker, Carl Cranke, Jack Penton, Paul Danik, Dane Leimbach, and Tom Penton. In the foreground is Larry Maiers, team manager (Jerry West photo).

and Danny Young. It was a disastrous year for the team, with Tom's bike catching fire before the first check on the first day. Team manager Larry Maiers was shattered, reporting that the foam seal around the air box had inexplicably ignited. Dane, Jack, and Danny won gold medals, and Eric won a bronze. Jack was top American and the Trophy Team finished sixth overall. Penton riders Gary Younkins and Rod Bush earned gold medals, and Drew Smith received a bronze. The event served to debut a new 125cc Penton, featuring a KTM-built, six-speed engine with magnesium cases, but it was the last year Penton would field a six-man American Trophy Team.

In 1976 Penton fielded the four-man American Silver Vase team at Zeltweg, Austria, featuring Jack, Tom, Carl, and Dane. It was a relatively easy event, but the level of competition was fierce. Despite the fact that every member of the team earned a gold medal, the U.S. Vase team still finished only in 4th place. The American Trophy Team—an odd collection of mixed brands—fell to 10th. Fourteen Penton riders earned gold medals.

In 1977 the ISDT returned to Czechoslovakia for a wet and difficult event. The U.S. Silver Vase team still included John Penton proteges: Jack Penton, Carl Cranke, Gary Younkins, and Rod Bush. Twenty-five Americans were on gold after the fifth day of the event. All but one lost their gold during the grueling sixth day. All of the Vase Team fell to silver, finishing 10th overall.

That big changes were in the works for Penton Imports was suggested by the fact that the bikes ridden by the Silver Vase Team in Czechoslovakia were branded Penton/KTM. It was the last time that Penton would appear as a factory brand in Six Days' competition, since, in 1978, the U.S. Silver Vase team was riding motorcycles simply branded KTM. The era of Penton motorcycles and Penton-trained American teams had come to an end. However, during the Penton's decade, the ISDT was not only the crucible from which Penton Imports refined a superior motorcycle, but also the source of international honor for many of America's young riders. Not counting the Belgians, Italians, Fins, Austrians, and Swedes who entered the Six

Days' on Penton motorcycles, not counting the Canadians who used Pentons, and not counting the European riders who rode KTM-branded mounts identical to Pentons, American competitors aboard reliable Pentons earned a total of 18 bronze, 17 silver, and 44 gold medals during the period.

As early as the mid-1970s, inflation and disruption in international money markets had taken its toll on Penton Imports. John Penton began to organize ISDT spectator tours to help offset the cost of funding a Trophy Team, yet he recalls that sometimes he still went in the hole as much as $30,000. Some would argue that such money is not out of line as a marketing expense for a company the size of Penton Imports. They would do well to remember that competing in the Six Days' is marketing of the riskiest kind. A good year brings prestige and value; a bad year brings shame and embarrassment, and luck is always the uncontrollable trump card. Consider, for example, the disastrous outcome of what should have been the Penton's finest hour, when the team rode for glory in front of their American fans at Dalton in 1973.

Larry Maiers, who managed Penton-mounted teams, acknowledges that for Penton Imports the ISDT represented a core marketing strategy, but he maintains that for John Penton the effort was fundamentally motivated by patriotism. He points out that when Penton Imports could ill afford it, John donated $30,000 to the AMA to help bring the ISDT to America. He says, "It wasn't just about Penton motorcycles. John wanted so badly for the United States to have a Trophy Team victory."

America has not yet won the ISDT World Trophy, but when a youthful team of American motocross riders devastated the competition in Belgium in 1981, John and Larry were there to witness the triumph. After the event, with the riders awash in excitement and champagne, John Penton approached Johnny O'Mara and Donny Hansen to offer his congratulations. Maiers says, "John was actually crying, and he said, 'I am so proud to be an American today. You guys have just done what we tried and tried so hard to do for so many years at the Six Days'.'"

14

The Dreadful Seventies

The American motorcycling boom of the 1960s was driven by prosperity and youthful optimism. It was a sad but fitting end to the decade that the so-called Summer of Love, officially celebrated by 500,000 people at Woodstock, New York in mid-August, 1969, turned to confusion, murder, and disillusionment at Altamont Speedway, near Livermore, California, on December 6th, when a fan at a Rolling Stones concert was killed by a member of the Hells Angels motorcycle gang. Well before this tragic event, the seeds of economic decline had already taken root, both in the motorcycle industry and the nation as a whole. The military buildup in Vietnam had started in 1965, and inflation of the U.S. dollar began to accelerate. As the decade ended and the 1970s arrived, America descended into a period of fear, pessimism, and economic chaos. It is sadly ironic that as the Penton became the most prominent name in off-road motorcycling, the forces were already at work that would limit the marque's life to a single decade. The product life of the Penton was meteoric: it would disappear as quickly as it had arrived.

Between 1967 (the year the Penton prototype was built) and 1978 (the year that the brand name was replaced by KTM), prices in America jumped by more than 80 percent. Consumer prices, advancing at an average annual rate of 7.4 percent during the period, represented roughly double the rate of inflation that had prevailed throughout the post-war period of 1950 to 1967. Inflation became the number one domestic policy issue of the 1970s, and it did not begin to abate until after President Reagan took office in January 1981. The extreme measures that were taken, primarily by President Nixon, to control inflation shook all of American society, and especially the motorcycle industry, which was largely an import business.

Acting under the authority of the Economic Stabilization Act of 1970, on August 16, 1971, Nixon implemented a wage and price freeze, enacted a tariff of up to 10 percent on imported materials and products, and effectively took America off the Gold Standard, announcing that the dollar would be allowed to fluctuate against foreign currencies and no longer have its value pegged to the price of gold, which had been fixed at a rate of $35 an ounce. These extreme measures were intended to blunt organized labor's efforts to keep wages ahead of the high rate of inflation, reduce or slow the growth of America's trade deficits, and protect its considerable gold reserves against possible plunder by large foreign creditors.

Confusion reigned. No one was sure how the new rules would be applied or enforced. *Cycle News* reported, "The changing value of the mark has caused the price of German-made goods to jump 13 percent since June; . . . the increase can't be passed on to the consumer, so in theory the distributor will have to absorb it." Although Penton motorcycles were manufactured in Austria, transactions between Penton Imports and KTM were conducted in German marks, making Penton especially vulnerable to a strengthening mark, a declining dollar, added tariffs, and a freeze on price increases. Fred Gilmore, of Penton's western distributorship, said, "The big Japanese firms can hold the line quite a while with their substantial resources, but many of the smaller distributors are working with no cushion." Chuck Swanson of Pabatco, importer of the Hodaka, echoed this concern: "We work on about a nine percent margin. If either the tariff or other factors force us to absorb more than nine percent, we'll be out of business." Tom Patton, who worked for Cemoto East, the importer of Bultaco, said simply, "It's a goddam mess!"

Nixon's gambit may have protected the government's gold reserves and reduced the foreign trade deficit, but it did not work with regard to inflation. At an average annual rate of 6.3 percent under his administration, it grew to 6.7 percent under the brief tenure of President Ford, then exploded to 9.4 percent under Jimmy Carter. In 1974, three years after the dollar was allowed to float and twice be officially devalued, *U.S. News and World Reports* stated, "After an era of unprecedented prosperity, Americans are starting to realize that the nation's economic machinery is badly out of whack. Inflation, only an occasional irritant since World War II, now is devouring family savings, putting familiar pleasure out of reach, and spreading insecurity." As one of the pleasures that more and more American families had discovered during the 1960s, motorcycling was in big trouble by the mid-70s. With fear of ever increasing prices for milk and mortgages, fewer consumers were inclined to spend money on expensive hobbies, especially those that required the consumption of gasoline.

With the outbreak of hostilities between Israel and the Arabs in 1973, the Arab oil producing nations implemented an oil embargo, followed by a 400 percent increase in oil prices, touching off the first of two so-called energy crises during the decade; first in 1974, then again in 1978. Motor sports organizations were asked to reduce consumption by 20 percent, and, fearing federal intervention, voluntary restrictions were put in place. The AMA and other sanctioning bodies reduced the length of championship events and proposed other measures designed to reduce fuel consumption. Although some in the motorcycle industry opportunistically tried to stimulate road bike sales by claiming that motorcycles are a fuel-conservative form of transportation, the argument just didn't wash. Real economic and business impediments notwithstanding for companies like Penton Imports, motorcycling was simply losing its popularity and public acceptance. By the time it debuted at the box office in 1971, *On Any Sunday* was practically a nostalgia film. Furthermore, products like the Honda CR125 and the Suzuki RM125 were becoming technically competitive with the European brands, and the Japanese had economic staying power.

With the market softening and the dollar continuing to decline against the Deutschmark, John Penton realized that between the time he ordered a shipment of motorcycles at a given dollar value, and the time he had to pay for that shipment in German marks, their real price in dollars had increased substantially. The same applied to much of the Hi-Point Accessories line as well, including boots, gloves, suspension parts, tires, and ignition components. About Nixon's new dollar *U.S. News and World Reports* stated in March, 1973, "It is a dollar that has no fixed value in terms of other paper currencies. And it is a dollar that, at this point, has floated to a further decline in purchasing power abroad . . . Prices of more and more imported products are going to be marked up, giving another nudge to inflation. Doing business overseas is going to be more complicated and expensive. Businessmen will find it more necessary to hedge against rising and falling currency values."

One result of freeing the dollar from a fixed price based on gold was that while the dollar fell, the price of gold increased. Soon it appeared that precious metals were the only commodity of real value, and more international businessmen began to invest in gold and silver as a possible hedge against fluctuating currencies. As a result, gold and silver prices inflated at an alarming rate, with gold rising to as high as $875 an ounce. Precious metals became even more unstable than the leading national currencies, but many people became caught up in the prospect of making or protecting wealth through the ownership of gold, silver, platinum, and gems. As late as 1978 *Business Week* published an article entitled "The Super Safety of Gold and Gems." As history would show, it was bad advice.

John Penton got caught up in the rush. Toward the end of his control of KTM motorcycle distribution in America, Penton began to invest heavily in silver. In 1976 he met Dave Rathbun, a broker with the Waldock Investment Company. John and Dave became good friends. While Dave's specialty was the grain futures market, John urged him to invest in silver on his behalf. Unfortunately, more than just international economic forces were at work in silver and silver futures. The notorious Texas Hunt brothers—Nelson Bunker, Lamar, and W.

Herbert—had begun to move to corner the silver market, and their phenomenal rate of acquisition set off a herd response and a buying frenzy that inflated the value of silver over 600 percent. For a while it looked like John Penton had found the solution to all his foreign currency problems, and at one point he opened a coin shop to buy silver. The frenzy was so great that people were bringing in coins, silver tea sets, candle holders, and anything sterling they could lay their hands on.

By early 1980 the Hunts owned two-thirds of the world's commercial silver, much of it purchased on margin. When it became suspected that they were attempting to corner and control the market, panic set in. Commodity exchanges put limits on buying silver contracts on margin, which in turn limited what the Hunts would be able to sell at inflated prices. Fearing the financial viability of the Hunts, on March 27, 1980, Bache Securities issued a $100 million margin call against the brothers. The bubble burst and the price of silver began to plunge. It was estimated that the Hunts lost $4 to $7 billion on paper, and perhaps over $1 billion in real money.

The Hunts, as it turned out, could afford it, but many people couldn't. John Penton was one of the many caught in the reversal, and he suffered substantial losses. It was a sorry way to end what had been a bitterly difficult decade for the motorcycle industry, and for Penton Imports especially. Despite this, John and Dave Rathbun remained good friends. Rathbun, also disillusioned by financial markets, left his brokerage, and, in September 1987, went to work for John Penton. In 1989 he was named president and CEO of Hi-Point, which, by that time, was only in the business of trailers and electronic ignitions. The rest had been sold to Malcolm Smith in 1987.

15

The Battle for Brand

At first, Erik Trunkenpolz had not been overly enthusiastic about John Penton's dream of a better off-road motorcycle. Although his company had created a promising Sachs-powered prototype sport motorcycle prior to 1967, it had little understanding of the potential of such a motorcycle, and uncertainty toward the American market where it's experience with the Hansa had been negative. Trunkenpolz thought it quite impossible to sell a $600 product against the Japanese in such a competitive market.

For the most part, KTM was a company that designed and built the rolling chassis on which it attached its nameplate, relying upon engines provided by other German and Austrian companies, including Puch, Rotax, and Sachs. It specialized in bicycles, scooters, and small transportational motorcycles, although it also dabbled in road racing with a prototype developed in collaboration with the Italian firm, MV Agusta. As Jack Penton describes it, KTM was a company that—prior to the arrival of John Penton—had a limited vision. He says, "You've got to understand that they were kind of like an Ohio company that is content to make and sell a product in neighboring states like Michigan, Pennsylvania, and Indiana. They had no global vision. They were interested primarily in selling their products in limited European markets; in Austria and to other German-speaking nations." Kalman Cseh, whose job it was to develop KTM's international markets, confirms, "At that time we knew America could be an important market, but we had no idea what kind of product to introduce there."

John Penton changed all that by aggressively developing a KTM-built motorcycle for the huge American market, and launching its name to worldwide prominence through exposure at the ISDT. The Penton-created motorcycle, also manufactured under the KTM brand in Europe as early as 1970, resulted in a steady growth in production for KTM, totaling over 70,000 vehicles between 1967 and 1977. KTM, which employed 280 workers when John Penton came to visit in 1967, steadily expanded its work force to 600 by 1978, largely as a result of the business generated by the Penton concept, both in America and Europe. Matt Weisman says, "John Penton was the salvation of KTM. Their main business had been little more than mopeds and bicycles, and he really put them in a position to succeed in the motorcycle business."

Weisman's opinion is supported by Friedrich Ehn's German-language book entitled *KTM: World Championship Marque from Austria,* which reports, "In 1970, profits rose over 10 percent to 165 million shillings ($6.6 million). This increase was due mainly to good export sales, because the domestic market declined slightly."

However, the relationship between John Penton and KTM was not always smooth, and John failed to adequately protect his interests by taking out patents or contracting with KTM for ownership of product concepts and designs. Everything was done with a handshake, often following tense and emotional arguments and turf wars. During his visits to Mattighofen, John would sometimes disappear for a day or two, planting word with someone that he was over in Graz, visiting Puch. This tactic drove Erik Trunkenpolz mad, since KTM and Puch were intense rivals in the Austrian motorcycle industry. In fact, the Penton/KTM relationship had become stressed as early as 1970 when Penton Imports briefly distributed Puchs in America. It was a tactic aimed at forcing KTM to commit serious funding and attention to development of a 175cc engine, but Erik Trunkenpolz no doubt saw it as a threat to KTM's whole future. In a move that had complex diplomatic overtones, the American Puch distributorship was transferred in 1971 to John's friend Fritz Dengel, who had also been a life-long friend of Kalman Cseh's father, and whom Cseh had known from childhood.

But the battle over the new 175cc Penton was not fully re-solved. John, who was free from his Husqvarna affiliation by 1972 and anxious to expand his product line and enhance its reputation, wanted the new engines to come to the United States under the Penton brand. They did not. Rather, they had a large KTM logo cast into the case. It appeared intentionally designed to be more prominent than the name on the gas tank, and this angered John. In retaliation, Penton Imports began to retrofit a Penton nameplate to the Sachs engines used on its 100 and 125cc models, arguing they had a right to do so since the engines had been totally remanufactured to Penton specifications.

This infuriated Erik Trunkenpolz, who entered into an all-out battle with John Penton for brand name prominence. Mo-torcycles identical to the Pentons built for America were pro-duced with KTM on the gas tank for markets all over Europe. Sometimes European riders rode Penton-branded bikes in the ISDT, but the factory made sure were they listed as KTMs in the official results. At one point the staff in Ohio opened a con-tainer of new Pentons to find a large "KTM" stenciled on the back of each seat. Today, Jack and Jeff laugh about the violent scene that ensued. Jeff says, "Dad was enraged. He had us run-ning around, trying to find something we could use to scrub the KTM logo off the seats." Jack adds, jokingly, "Dad would have chiseled the KTM letters off the engine case if he could have figured out how to do it."

Matters only got worse in 1975 when Trunkenpolz pro-vided Ted Lapadakis with KTM-branded motorcycles to dis-tribute in the western United States. Lapadakis, who owned Hercules Distributing, was an experienced importer who han-dled DKW, and other European motorcycles. He had the expe-rience and resources to represent a genuine threat to Penton Imports. It was Erik Trunkenpolz's way of flaunting the fact that John Penton had no contract for exclusive control of the

Team Pentons are readied for Six Days' competition at the Isle of Man in 1971. In the background is Dave Mungenast. Note bikes carrying the KTM logo; a battle for brand recognition had begun (Jerry West photo).

American market. Understandably, this action made John furious.

By 1975, KTM was assembling nearly 10,000 vehicles a year, and was developing stronger European markets. It had become abundantly clear that America provided a strong and reliable off-road market, and that economic forces and a declining dollar were militating heavily against a "middle man" operation, such as Penton Imports. Penton was struggling to maintain a profitable operation, and Erik Trunkenpolz knew it. John Penton knew that KTM was moving toward a takeover of its American distributorship. In the absence of any long-term relationship governed by a contract, John Penton was vulnerable.

Penton Imports had almost everything going against it except expertise. John says, "By 1975 they had a great product, but KTM still didn't have a clue how to market in America. They knew it, and we knew they knew it. If they had tried to duplicate our operation and put us all out on the street, they would not have lasted two seasons. Our security was our know-how and our staff, our reputation in the American market, and our relationship with our dealers. They needed us, and they knew it."

Unfortunately, the two men who had built a revolutionary motorcycle by successfully fighting and yelling their way through disagreements were no longer speaking to each other. Jack Lehto, who had left Husqvarna to return to Penton Imports in 1977, was approached by Mr. Trunkenpolz to facilitate a solution. He says, "Mr Trunkenpolz was very worried. He knew how inflation and the declining dollar were affecting us, and he was afraid the whole U.S. operation might collapse. He also was unhappy with the energy John was putting into his Hi-Point business, and he was afraid motorcycle sales would suffer. But Mr. Trunkenpolz did not want to slam the door on John and Ted. He understood what they had created and how important it had been to his company." John's opinion is that KTM could not have slammed the door. They might have tried, but he believes Trunkenpolz knew he could not make it in America without the support of the Penton marketing team.

The time was ripe to negotiate an orderly and seamless transition of the distributorship from Penton Imports to KTM. Lehto says, "I talked with John and tried to convey Mr. Trunkenpolz's point of view. The economy had put John's back up against the wall, and I think he realized that the survival of Penton Imports and the accessory business might depend upon getting rid of the motorcycles." In fact, John confided to Donna at the time, "I would be better off just to close it down, but I've got a lot of employees who depend upon Penton Imports for a pay check." Those experienced employees would also be the key to any future success KTM might have in America, so their well-being became a crucial factor in shifting ownership and control of the distributorship. Lehto continues, "We used the corporate model we had developed with Husqvarna in 1972. A new corporation was created, owned principally by KTM. John kept Penton Imports to continue sales of his Hi-Point products, and KTM bought from him some of the property and assets necessary to the motorcycle business." Some of the key employees, including Lehto and Bush, went with KTM. Furthermore, the Penton-developed, off-road wrecking crew, including Jack, remained intact, leaving the beneficial impression among the industry, dealers, and customers that it was business as usual for Penton and KTM in America.

At the ISDT in Czechoslovakia in 1977, an American Silver Vase team of Jack Penton, Gary Younkins, Rod Bush, and Carl Cranke were riding motorcycles branded Penton KTM, which seemed to signal the transition. In 1978 the Penton name was dropped entirely, making the motorcycles KTMs, but the American Trophy team still included the familiar names of Bush, Penton, and Leimbach, plus Kevin LaVoi, Jeff Hill, and Frank Gallo. All of the conflict and rivalry between Penton Imports and KTM had been kept behind the scenes, resulting in an arrangement to shift ownership of the American distributorship to the parent company while keeping most of the experienced marketing team intact. However, the fact that a great era had come to an end was illustrated symbolically at the 1978 ISDT in Sweden, where Tom Penton won his last gold medal . . . riding a Suzuki! Furthermore, in the same year that the Penton motorcycle ceased to be, John's mother, the family matriarch, Nina Musselman Penton, died on May 15th. It was a year of passage for John Penton, both personally and professionally.

John Penton is a man who does not like to lose. In this case, he lost to adverse economic forces, not to KTM. He recalls the loss as a time of confusing and mixed emotions. He was deeply saddened to see the Penton motorcycle come to an end, but he did not regret shedding its marketing responsibility. Importing with dollars against Deutschmarks had become a hopelessly difficult business in the 1970s. Economic forces were against anyone trying to trade in dollars, and the Japanese companies had come on strong with rapid off-road product development, using their greater resources to weather the international monetary crisis.

As for his relationship with KTM, the battle for brand recognition between John and Erik seems not to have done lasting damage on his memory of their mutual respect and affection. In 1989, when Trunkenpolz was almost too ill to see anyone, he chose to see John Penton. Dave Rathbun describes the scene: "We were invited to visit Mr. Trunkenpolz at his home. He had a big house that, in the little industrial town of Mattighofen, looked like the castle of a king. We went inside and were directed to a big, beautiful room, and at the other end was an old man, sitting in a bathrobe. It was like a scene from *The Godfather,* this old guy—obviously very ill—and John Penton, sitting in chairs and talking quietly for the longest time. Then we left, and within a week or two Mr. Trunkenpolz was dead."

Erik Trunkenpolz died on December 29, 1989. John Penton attributes his death in part to the stress of business problems and a struggle with others seeking control of the company. Penton has not forgotten their many conflicts, but these memories seem to have lost their emotional sting. In August 1998, John Penton and Lyle Lovett were the guests of honor at the national KTM dealer's meeting, held at the Rock and Roll Hall of Fame in Cleveland, Ohio. By this time, Rod Bush and his staff had reestablished KTM as a strong and viable force in the U.S. motorcycle industry, admirably holding their own against the powerful Japanese manufacturers. John spoke to the dealers that evening, marveling at what had been accomplished with product design, congratulating them on their success, and shedding tears when he spoke to them about his collaboration and friendship with Erik Trunkenpolz.

16

Accolades

John Penton is an international motorcycling legend, a fact that has been both officially and informally acknowledged many times over the past forty years. His first worldwide recognition came as a result of his U.S. transcontinental record run in 1959. That feat was part of a three-year series of extraordinary accomplishments that included thirteen AMA enduro championships. As a result, he appeared on the cover of *American Motorcycling* in October, 1958; on the cover of *Cycle Magazine* in August 1959; and received from the American Motorcyclist Association in March 1961, its title of Most Popular Male Rider. This was one of the most satisfying recognitions of John's career, primarily because of the company it placed him among. John was an enduro rider and considered an amateur motorcyclist. The AMA's Most Popular Male Rider title invariably went to professional racers like Joe Leonard, Dick Mann, and Bart Markel because of the great and frequent exposure they received in the motorcycle press. Since John's form of motorcycling was not considered glamorous, he had to overcome a certain amount of convention and prejudice to beat out the fast guys to win this prestigious award. John was beside himself just to be brought onstage in Daytona Beach to stand among the nation's top ten. He registered genuine astonishment and disbelief when they announced he was the winner. It netted him another cover on *American Motorcycling* in April 1961.

John Penton, the AMA's Most Popular Male Rider in 1960, shares the stage with fast company. Back row, left to right: Bruce Walters, George Roeder, Everett Brashear, Al Gunter, Dick Klamforth. Front row, left to right: Bart Markel, Carroll Resweber, Penton, and Dick Mann (Daytona International Speedway photo).

In addition, all of John's enduro victories of that active period were aboard his little 175cc NSU. As a result, the German factory awarded him the NSU Victorious Rider Award in September, 1960, declaring him "the most important NSU rider in America." The award had only been presented seven times over the company's long history, and John Penton was the only American ever to win it.

Shortly thereafter, Penton switched to the 250cc BMW as his endurance machine of choice, and on the strength of his 1959 BMW-mounted record run and his AMA endurance championships in 1962, the Munich-based factory gave him a similar "victory award" during his stay in Garmisch-Partenkirchen for the ISDT in September 1962. BMW's company magazine, the German language *BMW Journal,* declared, "Penton came

John Penton, the AMA's Most Popular Male Rider in 1960, sharing the spotlight with Joan Watson, his female counterpart (Daytona International Speedway photo).

over here from America with a BMW R27 to participate for the first time in the International Six Days' Trial, and he quickly found himself the uncrowned favorite of the public."

Undoubtedly the most remarkable of Penton's motorcycling recognitions was when *Cycle News* declared him "Motorcyclist of the Decade" in its January 9, 1980 issue. The publication described him, "A legend in his own time. A man whose exploits would and should fill a book. A man largely responsible for the upsurge in off-road riding in the seventies . . . A man who always has a twinkle in his eye and an idea churning around in his head. A man for all seasons. A motorcyclist. John Penton, *the* Motorcyclist of the Decade." John considers this title one of the great highlights of his life.

Not all of John Penton's accolades have come from motorcycling organizations. In October 1988 he was inducted into

John Penton at Daytona Beach in March, 1961, holding his trophy after being named the AMA's Most Popular Male Rider for 1960 (Daytona International Speedway photo).

The Amherst Schools Distinguished Alumni Gallery of Success. In accepting that prestigious honor, he stated, "Success does not come by setting records, accumulating wealth, establishing a business, or erecting a monument. People are the name of the game. To have success you must build upon the immortal mind with love, without prejudice or greed."

In 1997 KTM paid tribute to John Penton by licensing two limited-edition John Penton Signature 30th Anniversary models. The motorcycles bore a special crest displaying John's signature on the front fender. They sold for a premium price of $1000 over suggested retail, and included a briefcase, a shirt, a cap, and other memorabilia bearing John's signature. Only 150 copies were made of the 200cc model. Only five copies were made of the 125cc model.

Perhaps one of the most convincing examples of Penton's legendary status was the creation of the Penton Owners Group in February 1998. Few men have the honor of seeing their name on the gas tank, and fewer still have seen his customers spontaneously form an owners' group during his lifetime. By contrast, the Harley Owners Group was not created until fifty years after the deaths of the company founders, and even at that, it is an officially endorsed, factory-funded marketing tool—not a spontaneously created enthusiast organization. As such, the Penton Owners Group is as much a cult of personality as it is an organization designed to honor and perpetuate a brand of motorcycle.

On January 23, 1999, the Penton Owners Group hosted a party in Amherst to honor John Penton. The occasion was used to present John with his gold medal as an inductee into The Motorcycle Hall of Fame, and the City of Amherst delivered a proclamation declaring that date the City's "John Penton Day."

Some of John's fans even wax poetic in singing his praise. The following was written by Al Born, who rode on the official Penton team in 1968, and now serves on the board of the Penton Owners Group.

My Friend John

I have known John Penton since back on the day
That I became the owner of my first BSA.
That started a friendship that lasts still yet;
He's as interesting a person as I've ever met.
John began riding enduros back in his prime.
He was one of the best at staying on time.
Neither trees nor swamps could slow him down;
Once he started the engine, he "just went to town!"
Of the major enduros, he has won almost all.
Though he always went fast, sometimes he would fall.
But that only happened just once in a while,
Because he knew in his heart he had to make that last mile.
Then John built a cycle that bore his own name.
It took thousands of riders to glory and fame.
Tom, Jeff, and Jack; Dane, Leroy and Paul
Won many enduros, and just had a ball.

So, John's been inducted in the great Hall of Fame;
Autographs and photos are a part of his game.
He'll sign pictures, caps, t-shirts, and gas tanks too;
But don't stand too close, or he just might sign you.

As we achieve a better historical perspective on the Penton era, the commercial motorcycle media has developed a greater appreciation for the significance of the technical contributions of John Penton and his colleagues. For example, in November, 1999, *Dirt Bike* magazine inducted the 1972 125cc and 175cc Pentons into its Fifth Annual Hall of Fame. While these were quite different machines—one with the new KTM engine and the other retaining the original Sachs power plant—the '72 was a new motorcycle from the ground up, featuring the chrome moly frame and flat-sided fiberglass gas tank. *Dirt Bike* explains, "Enduro racer John Penton knew what he wanted in a racing dirt bike, and he had KTM build it. It was so on-target that Penton became a major force in competition dirt bikes. Penton's vision of the ideal dirt bike included all the things racers wanted. The amazing thing is, he built his dream bikes, and they changed the sport of off-road racing forever."

John Penton is a bit baffled by his celebrity status. In his mind he remains a working man from Amherst who is more comfortable in his green grubbies than donning a coat and tie to receive an award. However, in recent years he has found it necessary to keep a felt-tip pen at the ready to sign caps, tee shirts, posters, and Penton gas tanks owned by his enthusiastic fans. At AMA Vintage Motorcycle Days in July, 1999, people lined up at the Penton Owners Group pavilion to get his autograph. At one point, one of John's colleagues realized that many of the fans were eight or ten years old, and he said, "John, do you realize that you stopped making motorcycles ten years before some of these kids were born?" John registered a look of sudden surprise, and replied, "You're right! What do you suppose that's all about?"

A good example of this surprising phenomenon are the O'Reillys of Ottawa, Canada: John, 11; and Matthew, 9. Young John professes to love Penton motorcycles, despite the fact that he has never ridden one. He asserts, "They are reliable and they handle well." When asked how he knows this, young John replied, "Because my uncle says so, and he has six of them." The legend lives on!

Uncle Mike O'Reilly, 41, who has inducted his young nephews into the Cult of the Penton, says, "Nothing attracts attention like a Penton. When I'm towing one of my bikes, people give me the thumbs-up on the highway." Shaun, father of John and Matthew, adds, "It was the golden age of dirt biking. The Penton team—Jack, Jeff, Paul Danik—were my heroes. It's all part of the infectious enthusiasm that comes from John Penton."

When informed that the AMA had already decided to make John Penton the Grand Marshal at AMA Vintage Motorcycle Days 2000, the O'Reillys respond in unison, "We'll be there!"

They will be among many, many devoted fans of John Penton and his legendary motorcycle.

17

The Man and His Work

At 75, John Penton consistently does a day's work that would break younger men. The dealership and the motorcycle import operation have long since been sold to others. The farm and the remainder of Penton Imports are in the hands of nieces and nephews. But John is up early every day. He can be found waist deep in a hand-dug ditch, trying to improve drainage on the Penton land, or moving his huge collection of hand-hewn sandstones from one corner of the property to another, or working on broken tractors so others can keep the farm running efficiently. If you want to talk with him, you must either wait until after 10 p.m. or settle for the answering machine.

John Penton's various enterprises have gone through good times and bad times. There were times when he worked demonically because it was necessary to keep his companies afloat. This is not the case today. He says he is not a wealthy man, but describes himself as "comfortable." He could easily hire others to dig the ditches, move the stones, and fix the tractors. Today he works because he wants to.

In April, 1970, brother Ted described him thus in an article in *Motorcyclist* magazine, "John Penton is part man, part machine—and what percentage is machine I have never been able to determine. But it is a highly-tuned machine and the closest thing to perpetual motion I have ever known. He is always on the run and usually has a day's work done before the sun comes up." That same year John stated to an interviewer

John Penton under uncommon circumstances: at the desk, wearing a
necktie, circa 1973 (AMA photo).

from *Cycle News,* "Why do you want to sleep so much? Your
body can only use so much, and you can't store it up."

But John's capacity for work has not always been easy on
others. Similar to Henry Ford and other driven men with a
vision, sometimes his family and associates have strained under the pace. Jack found himself overseas at the age of 16, fac-
ing the pressure of riding on the American International Six
Days' Trophy Team. Brothers Jeff and Tom—also members of
the team—were only 18 and 20 respectively. When Tom went to
Vietnam where he loaded bombs 12 hours a day to feed the
voracious appetite of the rolling thunder squadrons of B-52s,
his first letter home said, "This stuff is easy because of how we
were raised."

Extended family member Rod Bush, who progressed from
a Penton enduro team rider in 1973 to the presidency of KTM
USA today, knows well the cost of the Penton work ethic. Bush
says, "We would work in the import business until closing time
on Friday, then jump in the van with our bikes and gear and
head off someplace several states away for a national enduro.

We would compete, then drive all night Sunday night and be back at work at 8 a.m. Monday morning. Ideas like 'comp time' were unthinkable around Penton Imports."

That John never allows himself to get too far from work is illustrated by an event that took place in the wilds of Wales. John, Donna, Mary, and her husband Frank had attended a Rotary International convention in Wales. At the end of the convention they got a rental car and headed out into the country, still wearing their good clothes. John and Frank were wearing coats and ties. Not understanding the Welsh language, they inadvertently filled the tank of their rental car with diesel fuel. When they tried to siphon it out they learned that the tank had baffles, and the only recourse was to remove the tank. Mary says, "John got out his suitcase and opened it up. I couldn't believe it. Right there was a set of his green grubbies. He stripped down to his skivvies in the parking lot, put on his work clothes, crawled under the car, and removed the fuel tank. Who else do you know would pack work clothes to go to a Rotary convention?"

For many years John Penton was a dedicated Rotarian, serving for a time as the president of Amherst Rotary. His workaday style was such a local legend that the club ruled that John would be fined if he ever showed up for a luncheon *not* wearing his green grubbies. The special rule applied even during his term as president of the local club. Perhaps John—a notorious creature of habit—thought the rule might apply in Wales as well!

Donna says, "It would kill John to slow down. He still gets up in the bucket of a front-end loader to prune trees." She laughs, "At least we made him quit sticking a ladder in the bucket so he could climb higher." She explains that work makes John happy, but it wasn't always that way. By the mid-1980s, punishment from the job and from the pegs of a motorcycle had turned him into a physical wreck. In 1990 he had both knees replaced with titanium parts. In 1997 he underwent radical back surgery that resulted in new carbon fiber disks and five of his lower vertebrae were held in place with an ugly cage of titanium scaffolding. Without it, he would be in a wheelchair. With it, he joyfully bends at the waist, demonstrating that he can get the tips of his fingers within two inches of his toes. "I have over 95 percent of my movement back," he proudly proclaims.

John also had major heart surgery in 1996, which he handled, again, in typical John Penton fashion. Trouble arose in 1995 when he had a mild stroke on an airplane about two hours out of Frankfurt, while traveling to Europe with Dane Leimbach and Dave Rathbun. Upon returning to the United States, he learned that he had a small hole in his heart that had been there since birth! Instead of taking medication (he did not like the side affects) in January 1996, he made an appointment with the Mayo Clinic in Minneapolis, and drove there alone. He immediately underwent surgery, and Donna came to the clinic to join him. Within three days he was out, and on his way back to Amherst, with Donna behind the wheel. Just south of Chicago, in the middle of the night, Donna told John she was too tired to continue. John, deciding he was feeling pretty good, got behind the wheel and drove the remaining 250 miles to Amherst. He says with a laugh, "I'll bet I'm the only guy to drive over 700 miles to Mayo's, get his heart taken out and repaired, and drive home again, all in less than a week's time." John doesn't seem to like much down time.

John's capacity for work is clearly linked with his attitude toward pain. Penton seems to believe that pain is a thing one simply ignores as long as there's another job to do. The stories of his ability to endure are legendary. Son Jack says, "One time at the Little Burr Enduro, Dad caught up with me at a check. He got off his motorcycle, came over to me, and in a very soft and controlled voice said, 'Jack, I really screwed up.' The way he said it made the hair stand up on the back of my neck. I knew something really bad had happened."

John had bailed off and broken four ribs. Jack said, "Come on, let's get you to an emergency room," and John replied, "Are you kidding? Give me your kidney belt." Jack was a fit and trim young man with a waist several inches smaller than John's. But John somehow stretched the kidney belt all the way around his rib cage, wheezing painfully as he latched it up. He remounted and finished the event. Jack just shakes his head and says, "And there was absolutely no reason to finish that run. He had nothing to gain by it. But not finishing a job he had started was just beyond his comprehension."

At an 80-mile enduro in Toledo in 1967, the riders had been warned of a spot on the trail where there were two steel cables that had been clearly marked as a hazard. With son Tom riding just behind him, John shot safely under the first cable, but forgot about the second and turned around to check on the safety of his son. When he turned back—traveling about 40 miles per hour—the second cable caught him diagonally across the face, down across his cheek and neck. Eyewitnesses claim he flipped more than once in the air. Doug Wilford, who was also on the scene, said, "If it had hit his windpipe instead of his jaw, I know it would have killed him. I helped him get up. I was going to lead him back to the club grounds, but he started racing again."

Workers at the subsequent checkpoints were utterly horrified by his appearance. They urged him to stop and get help, but John would get his card punched and hurry on. The organizers even sent the local police after him to forcibly stop him. But they never caught up with him. Incredibly, John finished the event.

Riding partner Al Born says, "I finished the run and there was John slumped over in the back of the van, his head hanging way down almost in his lap. I knew something was wrong and walked up to ask him how he was doing. He looked up and it was horrible. The side of his face looked like hamburger. It was all purple and wet with blood seeping through the skin, and there was this big pouch of skin under his eye that looked like it was full of water. He didn't know where he was, but he had finished third overall and second in his class. Then he insisted on driving the van back to Amherst that night."

In 1968 John broke his collarbone just days before he was scheduled to depart for the International Six Days' Trial in Italy. Nevertheless, he entered the event, and on the fifth day, he fell and opened a gash in his knee clear to the bone. The event physician patched him up with 32 stitches. The next day John finished the event and earned his bronze medal, but reopened the savage wound in the process. The doctor who had to stitch him up again expressed dismay and asked why he had continued to ride. John replied, "No one told me not to." The doctor just shook his head and said, "I didn't think we had to."

It is not that John ignores or does not believe in doctors. In fact, there are two physicians on the Leimbach side of the family, and John readily and gratefully credits the medical profession for saving, prolonging, and vastly improving the quality of his life. However, he seems to form his own opinions about when a doctor is called for based on his high threshold of pain. For example, he once splinted a finger with duct tape and popsicle sticks in order to finish an enduro, then later called his doctor to ask him how long he should keep the makeshift splint in place. On another occasion, he took it upon himself to reattach the crown of a tooth with super glue, only to end up with the tooth hopelessly stuck to his finger.

Others have said that John Penton's ability to ignore pain and concentrate on the task at hand is nearly inhuman. Jack reports, "When he finally stopped working long enough to get his knees fixed, they discovered that he had worn away three-eights of an inch of bone from the left knee, and three-quarters from the right. Can you imagine the pain you would have to endure over a long period of time to do that kind of damage?" The doctor told him, "Most people would have been crawling ten years ago."

Seven-times AMA National Enduro Champion Bill Baird once said that when John started an enduro, he seemed to undertake a process of self hypnosis, maintaining a kind of trance throughout the event. Baird says, "He would come to the starting line with his mouth real tight and this big-eyed stare on his face like an angry bull. Then he would take off and ride through anything, no matter what. I've gone through a section as fast as I thought humanly possible, and John would fly by me, just crashing through everything, taking down saplings as he went." Jack confirms, "John has the ability to concentrate 1000 percent on one thing. When he gets in that mode, nothing from the outside is able to get through to him." Dane Leimbach says, "I think John's concentration and ability to ignore pain is driven by his enthusiasm for whatever he is doing, whether or not it involves motorcycles. He's enthusiastic about everything he undertakes."

One-time BMW importer Michael Bondy, whose father, Alfred, set Penton Brothers up as a BMW dealer, says, "My father considered John Penton a superman. His determination was incredible." Bondy sites the transcontinental record run as an example, and adds, "How he won so many enduros aboard that little 250 BMW is beyond me. That motorcycle was never meant to win offroad, but he made it do it." Dave Duarte, who managed Penton West until it closed in 1990, says, "I don't know anyone who would dive deeper and harder than John to make something happen in the motorcycle business. His drive was incredible."

At times John Penton has expected as much from others. Rod Bush says, "We were at a national enduro in Illinois and I had broken a collarbone. For John, that just wasn't a big deal. When we were ready to go he said, 'I'm beat. It's your turn to drive.' Whining to John about driving a stick-shift van with a broken right collarbone just wasn't an option. It was agonizing every time I had to gear down for and gear up from a toll booth every ten miles coming through Chicago. Then it was back to work first thing Monday morning. I could barely find the time to get it looked at. That's just how it was, working for John Penton."

John Penton has worked hard his whole life, from cutting asparagus each spring morning as a child to digging ditches and moving stones today. But in recent years he has throttled back a bit and found time to better enjoy the company of people. He has become less obsessed with work and more appreciative of the fruits of his labors. He and Donna have begun to find peace in what they have accomplished.

If you ask John today why he works so hard, why he continues moving stones and digging ditches, he will promptly reply, "Because God gave me my health back." For John Penton it is a simple and obvious equation. Work is the currency with which we repay God for the blessings of a good body and a quick mind.

18

Legacy

John Penton once said to his son Jack, "Your life is only a series of experiences." In many cases, our experiences come from events driven by forces beyond our control. We make choices to direct our fate, but, at best, those choices only send us in the direction of the next experience. It was so with John Penton, whose landmark motorcycle was—in the midst of its commercial success—driven into history by a convulsive and unpredictable economy. It was an experience that John found beyond his control.

To create the illusion that we have control, and to make sense of what may seem unfortunate or unfair, we create mythology. Mythology is the grand plot we devise in retrospect. Although it may be fabricated, it is not false. It is a higher form of truth, and it is important. It gives us an understanding of our past and hope for our future, and it creates an ethical framework within which we make our choices. Those who struggle vigorously to make something positive of their life experiences become the men and women who loom large in that mythology. Of them we say, "They made a difference," and the differences they made we call their legacy.

John Penton looms large in America's motorcycling mythology. But how shall we understand his legacy while the myth is still unfolding? Perhaps there is no better way than to consider the opinions of the people who were part of it: those who were his peers and proteges during what became the most exciting and revolutionary quarter century in America's motorcycling history.

Bob Hicks, who was publisher of *Cycle Sport* and one of the guiding forces in the creation of the New England Trail Riders Association, was on hand to see the first Pentons when they arrived at Daytona, just after the Stone Mountain enduro in 1968. Today Hicks says, "John Penton is the pied piper of enduro riding. Before the advent of the Penton, you had to know how to modify a motorcycle to make it work. You had to know how to seal the electrics and make other changes to survive an enduro. Then the Penton arrived and invited everyone to join in. It made it possible to go buy a motorcycle that was ready to ride."

Jeff Penton, who rode his namesake motorcycles in three ISDTs and many AMA national championship enduros, says, "The Penton created a fresh, clean, family movement. John Penton introduced the public to off-road riding at an affordable price. He also actually created a new enduro class. What serious enduro rider competed on a 100 or a 125 before the Penton? The Penton not only caused serious competitors to move to the smallest classes, but they began to beat the big bikes at national enduros."

Paul Danik, whose first off-road motorcycle was a Penton and who later earned a gold medal aboard one at the ISDT, says, "Kids learned that at the amateur level you could do just about anything with a Penton. You could do scrambles, flat track, hill climbing, motocross, enduros—about anything. The Penton enabled a lot of people to enjoy motorcycling in ways they would never have thought of before."

Matt Weisman, who abandoned his own advertising agency to work for John Penton full time, says, "John took glamour to the amateur level. We created a program that gave kids riding Pentons a lot of recognition in advertisements and the company newsletter. He made a lot of kids feel good about themselves and about riding motorcycles."

Dane Leimbach, who earned ISDT gold on Penton Trophy Teams, says, "John Penton brought a sporting mentality to the motorcycle business. With most companies, it's about sales, and if they get involved in motorsports, it is mainly to drive sales. With Penton, sport came first and sales followed. We never said, 'It has to sell better.' We always said, 'It has to work better.' John put building a better product above selling a product."

Don Brown, an industry consultant who urged Husqvarna to introduce a small motorcycle in the early 1970s, says, "I tried to make my clients understand that if they didn't create brand loyalty with the kids, they wouldn't have them as customers when they got older. It would appear that John Penton was one of the first to understand and act on that concept."

Through his journalistic vision, Joe Parkhurst introduced American motorcycling to wider horizons during the same period when John Penton, Bud Ekins, and a few others were beginning to compete in Europe. Parkhurst says, "I was an admirer of John from the beginning because he, through his creativity and inventiveness, spearheaded the development of the dirt bike market in America. He pursued growth and expansion when others were content to leave well enough alone."

Jack Lehto, who entered the motorcycle industry as an employee of Penton Imports, managed the Husky ISDT team that won the Silver Vase for America in 1973, and eventually became president of Husqvarna's U.S. distributorship, says, "John Penton was a true visionary in our industry. His bike brought thousands of people into off-road motorcycling."

The legendary Malcolm Smith, who starred in *On Any Sunday,* rode with John on the American Silver Vase team at the ISDT in El Escorial in 1970, then served on the team that won the Silver Vase in the United States in 1973, says, "John Penton was always trying to make things better. He raised the standards for agile, lightweight, off-road motorcycles."

Jack Penton, who rode Pentons at the ISDT for nearly a decade, says, "John Penton created an enjoyable experience and pleasurable memories for tens of thousands of people. Hundreds of people have talked to me about their Penton experience, and I have yet to meet someone who does not remember it fondly."

Paul Dean, editorial director for *Cycle World,* who worked for Penton competitor Yankee Motors, says, "More than anyone else, John Penton helped make the U.S. a legitimate player in off-road endurance riding at an international level, thereby raising the acceptance and sophistication of American off-road competition to a new and higher level, driving dirt bike sales for everyone."

Tom Penton, who won six ISDT gold medals in eight events, says, "Penton Imports led the pack at developing and introducing the modern trail bike, making a superior machine available to the general population."

Kalman Cseh, who is in charge of KTM's export business, says, "The biggest contribution he made was causing KTM to go into the off-road business. He brought KTM into the business, and it became quite a big player, worldwide. We would not have thought of it."

Lars Larsson, who helped import Husqvarnas and rode Pentons and Huskies in the ISDT, says, "He brought devotion to motorcycling. He probably could have made a lot more money doing something else, but think of all of the people he helped in motorcycling!"

Dave Mungenast rode on the Husqvarna team with Malcolm Smith, Bud Ekins, and John Penton at the ISDT in Zachopane in 1967, the first of nine consecutive events during which he earned six medals. Mungenast says, "I can't think of any other American, living or dead, who has done as much for off-road motorcycling as John Penton. No one else has ever put as much of his life, his money, and his enthusiasm into off-road motorcycling."

Dick Burleson, eight-times AMA Enduro National Champion and winner of eight ISDT gold medals, says, "He's the guy who brought motorcycling into the current age. He was the pioneer who brought us the lightweight, reliable, raceable motorcycle."

Michael Bondy, one-time American BMW distributor, says, "He is an innovator. He deserves much of the credit for where KTM is today."

Rod Bush, who was an early Penton dealer and later a Penton Imports employee who rose to be president of KTM USA, says simply, "John Penton was a pioneer. He created an industry."

Kenny Roberts, who was AMA Grand National Champion in 1973 and '74, and 500cc Road Racing World Champion in 1978, '79, and '80, collaborated with John Penton to market Alpinestar boots, and assisted Penton Imports with the development of a KTM-powered short track racer. He says, "John Penton saw more than anyone else saw, more than most people in America at the time. He earned a big place in American motorcycle history and business. Unfortunately, there is only one John Penton."

When John Penton approached KTM in 1967, it was a small company assembling a few motorcycles using engines provided by other European manufacturers. His development of a superior off-road motorcycle helped change KTM to a strong competitor in the world-wide motorcyle market, possessing leading-edge design and engineering capabilities. Two examples of KTM's latest products are the 2000 model year 125SX racer (above) and the 250EXC (below) off-road bike.

19

Epilogue: Traveling with John

John Penton and Dane Leimbach picked me up at my home promptly at 6 p.m. on September 30th, 1999, towing a new Hi-Point trailer filled with motorcycles. We were on our way to the 3rd annual Leroy Winters Six Days' Reunion in Ft. Smith, Arkansas. It seemed an odd time of day to begin a nonstop, 850-mile trip, but for John Penton it is business as usual. For years, John has driven nonstop to all points in the United States. In April, 1999, he and Penton Owners Group President Al Buehner drove from Amherst straight through to Sonoma, California, taking a three-state detour due to snow in the Rockies, to attend AMA Vintage Motorcycle Days. For two people, that was dead easy. With three people to drive, our trip was to be a piece of cake.

When John drives solo, he may pull off to take a nap at the wheel every 15 hours or so. For companionship he places a basket of apples and plums, personally picked from his own orchard, next to the driver's seat. He knows the interstate highway system better than the guts of a Sachs gear box, and every trip he undertakes is plotted out on an invisible route sheet in his head, hour by hour, like a national enduro. He knows exactly where he will stop for fuel and where he likes the way they maintain the bathrooms. While he may stop for road food from time to time, for the most part his Amherst plums and apples sustain him.

For many years Penton personally delivered Hi-Point trailers to dealers and customers all over America, piloting a Cycle

Liner that had been chopped down to a flat bed, carrying three trailers at a time. Hi-Point Trailers manager Dave Rathbun used his delivery-boy boss to sell lots of trailers. He explains, "If a dealer ordered a trailer, I would say, 'Hey, you take two and I'll have John Penton deliver them personally. If you want, he'll even autograph them.'" Rathbun laughs, "Of course, John was going to deliver them anyway, but they didn't know that! I sold more trailers, and they ended up feeling really special."

In the dead of night we whizzed through the nearly vacant freeways of Louisville, Bowling Green, Nashville, and Memphis, never taking the engine off cruise control. Near dawn we were passing through Little Rock, and traffic was just starting to build. "See this! See this!," John says with great satisfaction, "An hour later and we would be in a hell of a mess. We'd be down to a crawl through here." His enduro clock was working, and he had timed it perfectly. We passed Check Point Little Rock without delay. We pulled into Byrd's Camp Ground just east of Ft. Smith, just as old friends and companions are rolling out of their tents and campers to greet the day. John was energized, and he wouldn't take a nap until he had hailed and spoken at length with practically everyone on the property.

While everyone is welcome to the Six Days' Reunion, the stars of the event are ISDT veterans. Dave Mungenast, Mike Lewis, Chris Carter, Doug Wilford, Paul Danik, Jake Fisher, Jeff Fredette, John Smith, Jack Penton, Dwight Rudder, Fred Cameron, Dane Leimbach, and John Penton are there. So is Tommy McDermott, the first American to win Six Days' gold. There are vintage bikes and vintage riders, and the influence of John Penton is evident everywhere: nearly a third of the motorcycles entered, and fully half of those entered in the vintage class carry "Penton" on their gas tanks. Several other Pentons have been brought just for display, and Paul Danik proudly exhibits a cutaway Penton Sachs engine. Riders carefully don moth-eaten, decades-old Penton jerseys and crusty, threadbare Hi-Point pants. There is obvious pride among the owners of Pentons, and abundant goodwill toward the man who created the marque over 30 years ago. Even the old enduro soldiers who have known John for decades seek autographs on Penton shirts and caps, allegedly for their grandkids.

The story of the marque can be seen as a story of travel, as John's odyssey. Whatever fears or naivete that may have limited the vision of a young man from Amherst were worn away by his years in the Merchant Marine, from Ohio to Europe to Asia. With his return to Amherst he brought experiences that broadened his horizon beyond Ohio farm country, and increased his confidence to cope with other cultures. Then came his exploration of America and Mexico aboard motorcycles, and his forays into Canada to earn off-road riding championships. He journeyed—often by motorcycle—to the Jack Pine and other prestigious enduros where he discovered his need for a better off-road motorcycle, for better gear, for better boots.

Victories at the Jack Pine, the Little Burr, the Sandy Lane, the Alligator, and Stone Mountain led him to foreign lands, to places with strange names like Zachopane, San Pellegrino, El Escorial, Garmisch-Partenkirchen, Zeltweg, Spindleruv Mlyn, Povazska Bystrica, to the mother of all enduros, the International Six Days' Trial. There he refined his vision of a better motorcycle, and discovered the resources to make it a reality. When John's European chapter began, the prop-driven Constellation was still the fastest way to cross the pond, and over the next three decades he made that trip six to eight times a year.

In the course of his odyssey, Penton helped revolutionize motorcycling, alter the aspirations of American riders, redefine standards of performance and quality in off-road motorcycling, and internationalize a sport and an industry. He influenced trends that enriched tens of thousands of people, both emotionally and materially. He turned local mud-runners into world-class champions, and provided the means for countless young people to experience the joy of motorcycling. Some of these world-beaters became quite wealthy in the process.

But the ultimate destination of every odyssey is home, and in a way John Penton never really left Amherst. While he is fiercely proud of his name and his family's accomplishments, John Penton remains humble and self-effacing. Like a security

John Penton, riding his namesake motorcycle at a southern Ohio two-day trial in 1973 (Rick Kocks photo).

blanket and a reminder of his roots, he always packs his green grubbies for his jaunts to Europe. His style remains unaffected, an agrarian worker who—between meetings with captains of industry—has found time to patiently tend the orchards behind his home on North Ridge Road, just a few hundred yards from both the house in which he was born and the chicken coop in which he launched his career. He seems to experience as much pride toward the yield of his tomato patch as he does toward the creation of one of the world's best off-road motorcycles. Like the box of apples and plums that invariably accompany him on his nonstop trips across America, John Penton has never left behind the values, the work ethic, and the relentless drive to finish a task that he learned as a boy growing up in Amherst, Ohio.

My plans called for me to travel on to Oklahoma after the Six Days' Reunion, rather than return to Ohio. Unfortunately,

Dane suffered an injury during the event, leaving John to handle the driving alone. I say to John, with some concern, "Will you be okay?" John scoffs, "Are you kidding?!" I am suddenly embarrassed. I realize I have sounded patronizing, and this is unacceptable. I have forgotten that I am talking to John Penton, the traveler, the ocean voyager, the midnight driver, the coast-to-coast rider, the worldwide flyer. It is as foolish as asking Odysseus if he knows how to trim a sail.

Following his marathon trip with Penton to California early in 1999, Al Buehner said, "John doesn't live in the past. He lives today. He lives in the present, and he thinks about the future."

Appendix A

A Penton Chronology

1891 Nina Musselman is born, June 18th.

1893 Harold Penton is born in Detroit.

1917 Harold and Nina are married and move to Amherst, June 18th.

1918 Ike is born, May 14th.

1919 Ted is born, June 22nd.

1921 Hank is born, June 17th.

1922 Mary is born, December 3rd.

1925 John is born, August 19th.

1927 Patricia is born, October 25th.

1929 Bill is born, April 3rd.

1936 Ike buys a 1933 Harley-Davidson.

1938 Harold dies, January 4th.

1943 John joins the Merchant Marine.

1945 John joins the Navy.

1946 John is discharged from Navy.

1948 Penton brothers open a machine shop. Bill and John enter the Jack Pine for the first time, John riding a Harley Knucklehead, and Bill riding a Harley WLA.

1949 John and Katherine Marks are married, June 26th. John finishes 2nd at the Jack Pine, riding a BSA.

1950 Penton Brothers Motorcycle Agency is established. Tom is born, May 19th.

1951 Penton Brothers Motorcycle Agency is incorporated, July 2nd. Dane Leimbach is born, September 18th.

1952 Jeff is born, April 15th. Laura Hochenedel is born, November 8th.

1954 Jack is born, July 16th. Bill wins the Jack Pine, riding a BSA. Amherst Meadowlarks Motorcycle Club is incorporated, November 17th.

1955 Barbara Hochenedel is born, November 18th.

1957 Katherine Penton is diagnosed with MS. Brad Hochenedel is born, November 18th.

1958 Katherine dies, February 28th. John wins the Ohio State Championship enduro, riding a BSA. John rides an NSU to victory at Stone Mountain, the Alligator, Little Burr, Jack Pine, and the Corduroy. In October, John appears on the cover of *American Motorcycling*. In October and November, John rides a BMW to Mexico.

1959 John wins the Little Burr and Corduroy, riding an NSU. June 8 thru 10, John sets a coast-to-coast record riding a BMW. Bob Hochenedel dies, July 19th. In August, John appears on the cover of *Cycle Magazine*. Ted Leimbach is born, February 15th.

1960 John rides an NSU to victory at the Jack Pine, Sandy Lane, Corduroy, and Ball and Chain Enduros. John and Donna Hochenedel are married, May 27th. John receives the NSU Victorious Rider Award, September 28th.

1961 John wins the Little Burr on an NSU. John is named the AMA's Most Popular Male Rider. In April, John appears on the cover of *American Motorcycling*. Tim is born, June 23rd. John wins the Corduroy on a BMW.

1962 John rides a BMW to victory at Little Burr, Sandy Lane, and Schuyler County enduros. The new dealership is opened on Cooper-Foster Road. Friend Jack Mercer challenges John to build a motorcycle. John rides a BMW in the ISDT, Garmisch-Partenkirchen, West Germany. In December, John appears on the cover of *Cycle World* magazine.

1963 John wins the Corduroy on a BMW.

1964 John rides a BMW to victory at the Stone Mountain, Alligator, and Jack Pine Enduros. Tom and Jeff get their first motorcycle.

1965 John rides a BMW at the ISDT, Isle of Man, Great Britain. Chuck and Sharon Clayton start *Cycle News West.* Jack and Laura get their first motorcycle. Kathie (Stashick) Towne goes to work for Penton Honda. Ralph Haslage joins Penton Honda.

1966 Doug Wilford goes to work for Penton Brothers. John rides a BMW at the ISDT in Sweden. Brad Hochenedel dies, November 18th. Elmer Towne joins Penton Honda.

1967 John rides a Husqvarna to victory at the Alligator, Little Burr, and Jack Pine. Penton becomes a Husqvarna distributor for the eastern United States. *State Motorcycle News* is established. John rides a Husky at the ISDT at Zachopane, Poland. John meets Erik Trunkenpolz. In December, the Penton prototype arrives in Amherst.

1968 The first Pentons arrive in America on March 7th. They debut at Stone Mountain on March 10th. In April, John sells State Motorcycle News to Chuck and Sharon Clayton. John, the only finisher at the Little Burr, rides a Husqvarna. John wins the Berkshire International Trial aboard a Husky and the Penton brand wins the Team Trophy. John Penton rides a Penton at the ISDT at San Pellegrino, Italy. Tom rides his first ISDT. Penton fields an ISDT Silver Vase Team. John co-promotes the Inter-Am at New Philadelphia, Ohio. Penton wins the Team Trophy at the Corduroy. Kathie Staschick and Elmer Towne are married.

1969 John rides a Husky to victory at Alligator, Burr Oak, and Jack Pine, and wins the AMA Enduro Grand National Championship. The Penton brand wins five classes at Jack Pine. John rides a Penton at the ISDT at Garmisch-Partenkirchen, Germany. Penton fields a Silver Vase Team. Matt Weisman joins Penton Imports. 100 and 125cc Pentons become available as both enduro and motocross models. Hi-Point Accessories is launched.

1970 Penton Imports is incorporated, April 30th. John rides a Husky at his last ISDT at El Escorial, Spain. Jeff and Jack ride their first ISDT. Penton fields a Silver Vase Team. Dale Barris goes to work for Penton Brothers Motorcycle Agency. Alpinestar boots are introduced under the Hi-Point brand name.

1971 John wins the Stone Mountain on a Husky. Penton fields an ISDT Trophy Team at Isle of Man. Dane Leimbach rides his first ISDT. Jack Lehto goes to work for John Penton as a Husqvarna representative. The new corporation becomes partially owned by Husqvarna set up as U.S. a distributorship. *On Any Sunday* is released.

1972 The new Husqvarna distributorship takes over, January 1st. Jack Lehto leaves Penton to become CEO of the new Husqvarna distributorship. 175cc Penton Jackpiner model is introduced, featuring a new KTM engine. Penton Mud Lark trials bike are introduced, featuring 125cc and 152cc Sachs engines. Larry Maiers joins Penton Imports. Penton fields an ISDT Trophy Team at Spindleruv Mlyn, Czechoslovakia, and the team wins the Watling Trophy.

1973 Rod Bush opens a Penton dealership and rides for the Penton enduro team. Penton fields a Trophy Team in the United States ISDT. Doug Wilford leaves Penton Imports in November.

1974 250cc Penton Hare Scrambler is introduced. Penton fields an ISDT Trophy Team at Camerino, Italy. KTM wins the 250cc motocross world championship. Husqvarna finalizes buyout of the U.S. distributorship.

1975 New 125cc KTM engine is introduced. Penton fields an ISDT Trophy Team at Isle of Man. 400cc Penton Mint 400 is introduced. In October, Ted Penton is injured in a street accident.

1976 Rod Bush goes to work for Penton Imports. Penton fields an ISDT Silver Vase Team at Zeltweg, Austria. Penton short track racer is introduced. John meets Dave Rathbun and begins to trade in silver.

1977 Penton fields an ISDT Silver Vase team at Povaska Bystrica, Czechoslovakia. Ted Leimbach rides his first ISDT. The Pentons at the ISDT are re-branded Penton KTM. Jack Lehto goes to work for Penton. KTM buys out the U.S. distributorship, effective year end.

1978 The Penton name is removed from motorcycles, and the first KTM ads appear in the American press. Nina Musselman Penton dies, May 15th. Jack Lehto is named CEO of KTM USA.

1980 *Cycle News* declares John Penton "Motorcyclist of the Decade." The silver markets collapse on March 27th. Ted Leimbach dies September 24th.

1982 Rod Bush becomes the national sales manager for KTM USA.

1983 Penton Central is closed.

1984 Larry Maiers leaves Penton Imports. Kathie and Elmer Towne leave Penton Imports. Hi-Point Trailer Company is launched.

1986 Matt Weisman leaves Penton Imports in December. Kathie Towne joins KTM USA.

1987 Hi-Point Accessories is sold to Malcolm Smith. The Penton Brothers dealership is sold to Dale Barris. Rod Bush becomes the president of KTM USA. Dave Rathbun goes to work for Hi-Point Trailers.

1988 John is inducted into The Amherst Schools Distinguished Alumni Gallery of Success. Jack Lehto leaves KTM USA.

1989 Erik Trunkenpolz dies, December 29th.

1990 John has knee surgery.

1991 Ted dies, January 11th. Bill dies, March 8th.

1994 Hank dies, December 25th.

1996 John has heart surgery.

1997 John has back surgery. KTM introduces 125cc and 200cc John Penton Signature 30th Anniversary special edition motorcycles.

1998 The Penton Owners Group is founded, February 26th. Hi-Point Trailers is sold. John is inducted into The Motorcycle Hall of Fame.

1999 The Mayor of Amherst declares January 23rd "John Penton Day." The AMA announces that John Penton will be the Grand Marshal at the AMA Vintage Motorcycle Days, 2000, and that Penton will be a commemorative marque.

Appendix B

Penton Rider Performance at the International Six Days' Trial

The following is a record of medals earned by American team riders at the International Six Days' Trial from 1968 through 1977. This record does not include European riders competing on Pentons or KTMs during the period.

1968: San Pellegrino Terme, Italy
Silver Medal:
   Tom Penton
Bronze Medal:
   Wolf Jackson
   Dave Mungenast
   John Penton

1969: Garmisch-Partenkirchen, West Germany
Silver Medal:
   Ronald Bohn
   Dave Mungenast
   John Penton
   Leroy Winters
Bronze Medal:
   Bud Green

1970: San Lorenzo del Escorial, Spain
Gold Medal:
   Jeff Penton
   Tom Penton

Silver Medal:
  Gene Cannady
Bronze Medal:
  Mike Lewis
  Jack Penton
  Doug Wilford

1971: Isle of Man, Great Britain
Gold Medal:
  Gene Cannady
  Lars Larsson
  Dane Leimbach
  Dave Mungenast
  Jack Penton
  Tom Penton
Silver Medal:
  Mike Lewis

1972: Spindleruv Mlyn, Czechoslovakia
Gold Medal:
  Gene Cannady
  Carl Cranke
  Dane Leimbach
  Jeff Penton
  Bill Uhl
Silver Medal:
  Jim Hollander
  Jack Penton
Bronze Medal:
  Dick Burleson

1973: Dalton, Massachusetts, United States
Gold Medal:
  Joe Barker
  Carl Cranke
  Paul Danik
  Dane Leimbach
  Jack Penton
  Bill Uhl
  Doug Wilford

Silver Medal:
    Tom Penton
Bronze Medal:
    Jeff Penton

1974: Camerino, Italy
Gold Medal:
    Carl Cranke
    Jack Penton
    Tom Penton
Silver Medal:
    Joe Barker
    Paul Danik
    Eric Jensen
Bronze Medal:
    Dane Leimbach
    Bob Ismalof
    Ron Lamastus
    Danny Young

1975: Isle of Man, Great Britain
Gold Medal:
    Rod Bush
    Carl Cranke
    Dane Leimbach
    Jack Penton
    Danny Young
    Gary Younkins
Bronze Medal:
    Eric Jensen
    Drew Smith

1976: Zeltweg, Austria
Gold Medal:
    Rod Bush
    Carl Cranke
    Donald Cichocki
    Frank Gallo
    Bill Geier

Jeff Gerber
Jeff Hill
Harry Heilemann
Eric Jensen
Dane Leimbach
Jack Penton
Tom Penton
Dennis Vandecar
Gary Younkins
Bronze Medal:
Rick Weathersbee

1977: Povazska Bystrica, Czechoslovakia
Gold Medal:
Tom Penton
Silver Medal:
Rod Bush
Carl Cranke
Jack Penton
Gary Younkins
Bronze Medal:
Kevin Lavoi
Ted Leimbach

Medal Count; 1968 through 1977
44 Gold, 17 Silver, 18 Bronze

Appendix C

By Patricia Penton Leimbach

John Penton's younger sister, Patricia Leimbach, is an accomplished writer whose columns appear in *The Chronicle Telegram* of Elyria, Ohio, and *The Farm Journal.* Her work has been anthologized in three volumes, *A Thread of Blue Denim, All My Meadows,* and *A Harvest of Bittersweet,* published by Harper and Row. While the theme of her work is life on the farm, on occasion she has written about the role of motorcycles within her family. Like their Penton cousins, her sons became world-class off-road competitors. Reprinted below, with permission, are three selections: "My Mother the Motorcyclist," about her own experience in learning to ride, "Big John," about her brother in Europe, and "Requiem," the haunting tale of the death of her son, ISDT gold medallist Ted Leimbach.

My Mother the Motorcyclist

I suppose I heard it once too often. "You mean you belong to that motorcycling Penton family and you never rode a motorcycle?" I decided it was time to change all that.

The kids gave me what you might call a "crash course" in trail riding. It started, like all courses, with basic advice:

"You'll have to wear long pants, Aunt Pat, and shoes and socks." My nephew was passing on the safety rules he'd been taught, but I smiled at the unlikely prospect of Aunt Pat's doing an "endo" on the trail. I changed my shorts and shoes, hoping he wouldn't notice if I went sockless.

Tim loaned me a helmet and buckled it under my chin, much as I used to zip his little jackets or tie his shoes on his frequent visits to End o' Way through the years. Then he showed me the controls from starter switch to foot brake, gave me one long sentence's worth of instruction, and turned his precious trail bike over to me. (My sons wouldn't trust me with theirs—the ones I "own.")

I cranked it a couple of times and nothing happened. Ted came riding alongside me at that moment.

"I think you better turn on the switch, Mom," he said. It started. I twisted the throttle, released the clutch, and was off on the grand adventure, clutching the handlegrips in that zoom-zoom posture, wind pushing my chest, pavement racing past under my feet, one with all the black-jacketed heroes of motorcycle legend—me and Marlon Brando, me and Steve McQueen, me and Evel Knievel.

Delusions of grandeur . . . and I wasn't even out of low gear. I shifted roughly to second, then to third. I was overtaken about then by Tim and Ted. "Are you using the clutch?" one hollered. "Doesn't sound like you are." There was going to be no sloppy riding with these guys.

My ankle was sending little messages to my brain saying, "There's something very hot down here that's hostile to the anklebone."

"Hey!" I shouted, "I want to go back to the house and get some socks." Tim refrained from I-told-you-so's.

An hour later, high work shoes over my ankle burns, I was speeding with quite some confidence around the motocross course, up and down hillocks, over the ruts and roughs, shifting 'er up and down, leaning into the curves, standing on the pegs—a real hotshot!

One more hour and there I was on Peasley Hill descending a shale ridge at 45 degrees between two knee-deep ruts when— Pow! I wiped out.

Tim had overlooked an important part of the gear. One needs a soft shirt to sop up the blood. I clapped my hand over my face to stem the bleeding. The boys came running and plied me with anxious questions.

"I'm fine," I assured them, unfolding myself and ignoring numerous sensory messages, all of which underscored a Leimbach maxim: "Don't tell me about your hero wounds."

"But what did I do to the bike? And I've lost my wedding ring." Someplace along the way I had switched bikes with Tim and was riding my son's. He was going to be furious. Something told me, too, that when I came limping in, dripping blood from a motorcycle accident, I wouldn't really need the wedding ring.

"The bike's OK, Aunt Pat. You just bent the fender a little. Gee, I've never seen anyone like you!" It was an ambiguous compliment, but it soothed my wounded ego.

I finally found my ring, bathed my dirty face in Chance Creek, and idled the cycle home around the roadway, avoiding the tough, steep river valley. As I entered the house, Paul gave me a disgusted glance and said, "What did you do to the cycle?"

Surprisingly, Orrin leaped to my defense. "Nothing. It's fine!" (God bless little boys with foolhardy mothers!)

I dropped Tim off at his home that evening, hoping to avoid my brother John, who is a national legend in motorcycle circles, the dogged survivor of thousands of cuts, bruises, scrapes, and fractures. As luck would have it, there he stood with a lawn mower right next to the driveway.

"What in the hell did you do to your face?" he asked.

"Oh . . . I, ah . . . had a little skirmish on a motorcycle," I said.

"When are you going to grow up?" he said, shaking his head and releasing me into the select fraternity of the initiated.

That was a couple weeks ago and now nothing's the same . . .

"What's happened to your mom?" say the young bucks sitting around the front lawn as I hobble past.

"Aw, she wiped out over on Peasley Hill," my sons say with a tone in their voices I never heard before.

In the grocery I encounter a familiar-looking young girl with a huge burn on her leg. "What in Sam Hill happened to your leg?" I ask.

"Motorcycle exhaust," she says. "What happened to you?"

"Motorcycle" I say, in the smug manner of those whose blood has mingled in secret ritual.

Big John

People seldom take you seriously when you talk about motorcycling—a reckless pastime for the immature or the insane, but in my family—the Penton family—Motorcycling is capitalized, and it's serious business. So . . . on holidays we sit at the feet of Brother John (or Papa John, Uncle John, Big John, according to your relationship), and we listen to The Gospel According to the Motorcycle Business.

Starting about 10 years ago as a folk hero among motorcycle racers, Brother John harnessed his talents as mechanic, machinist, innovator, go-getter, and with considerable help from his brothers developed a winning motorcycle that bears his name. It is manufactured in Austria, then imported and distributed nationwide through the dealerships Brother John and Ted organized.

Their motorcycle business involves the convoluted worlds of industry, economics, law, transportation, labor relations, public relations, and sport. I find the whole thing fascinating, so I listen and ask questions, and ponder the world as Big John discovers and shares it, tempering my judgments on the basis of my own experience. It is John and the international business that intrigues me the most. As an importer he does a lot of poking around in out-of-the-way corners of Europe, a lot of bargaining, bickering, shouting, negotiating, socializing, discovering.

As a negotiator Johnny is no Henry Kissinger. He is, in fact, one small, solid lump of incongruity. Short and stocky, looking very much like—what else?—an old motorcycle hero, he stomps on and off airplanes heavily weighted with briefcases full of gear shift levers and assorted spare parts.

He's not particularly tactful, diplomatic, or gifted in language, but in the way that candor and honesty translate, he is altogether disarming and enjoys great success. He and his Austrian factory owner rant and rave and tear their hair in separate languages. They don't speak for a day, then fall on each other's necks, shake hands, and part like brothers—business mission accomplished.

Last week Brother John did seven countries in nine days, so on the Fourth of July he was still effervescing with his experiences. When John encounters something unique, he brings it back like a shiny pearl in the palm of the hand to share and delight over, as though no one else ever found anything to compare, and he convinces me every time.

"Last week I was sitting in a restaurant in Venice . . ." (Sitting there straddling a picnic bench as he tells it, wearing work clothes, pant legs rolled to the knees, white socks drooping, it seems an unlikely story.) "And they brought out this steaming plastic bag, split it open, and there lay two ugly steamed fish with their sunken eyes, their slimy-looking skin. Some big delicacy! I thought I'd vomit."

"Did you eat it?" I asked.

"Heck no. I had a club sandwich, like over at Friendly's." Big John in Venice.

Once it was a castle ruin on the Danube he'd found and thought everyone should see. (Eventually he arranged that many of us could.) Once he found a wonderful little boot factory on an obscure back street in a tiny Italian village. Another time, a wooden shoe factory in a ski village. Once, a parts factory in an abandoned palace, a suit works in Germany, sewing machines in Sweden, an electronic marvel in Madrid.

This trip he'd stopped through Denmark to visit Brother Bill's Danish in-laws and he'd seen amazing pigs bred with two extra ribs!

Once he fell asleep on a train, missed his stop, and debarked in the middle of nowhere in Yugoslavia, where he had a heck of a time explaining to the station master that he neither wanted nor needed any "deeners." He wasn't hungry. It finally came through to John that he was talking about units of Yugoslavian money, "dinars." Using his well-developed language of pantomime, he got himself on a train in the opposite direction and caught a plane back to civilization.

Non-drinking, non-smoking, no-nonsense Papa John does not fit the picture of hail fellow, well met. I can see him in a

Belgian beer hall, his eyes glazed over, his face in semi-consciousness, wishing he were under an eiderdown dreaming of 6:00 a.m. and another exciting day in the motorcycle business. The Europeans, dedicated socializers, forgive him his dreary cop-outs, because his dedication to business is their bread and butter and they esteem him highly.

One frigid day last winter, I caught sight of Uncle John at the local motorcycle track bundled in his raunchy brown stocking cap and a ratty old ski jacket held together at the front with a safety pin. (I recognized it as one of my husband's that I'd thrown away two years ago.) Nobody would have pegged him for an international businessman who sits at a polished mahogany table in Vienna, flanked by interpreters, bankers, tax lawyers, accountants, and stodgy European business executives.

I think the reason Big John gets along so well abroad is that he's the most uncommonly common guy to come across from the States since Benjamin Franklin.

Requiem

When Ted was a lad and you asked him the "when you grow up" question, he'd say, "I'm going to race motorcycles till I'm too old, and then I'm going to farm." In a somewhat complicated way he managed to pursue those dual goals.

During the winter and spring quarters of his junior year at Ohio State he flew on successive weekends to Georgia, Michigan, California, Virginia, Oklahoma, Oregon, Washington, and Alabama to race. During the week, he grappled with agronomy, marketing, and ag economics. All summer he would mow and cultivate, pick and pack until four o'clock, then go off to work on a motorcycle engine till after midnight. The culmination of all this winter, spring, and summer endeavor was to be the International Six Days' Race in France in September.

This is a long grueling race threaded through mountains and valleys, riverbeds and fire trails, thickets and meadows. The riders depart four to a minute at 7:00 each morning and cover 200 or more miles each day. If a rider can maintain a constant pace, keep his machine together, and stay on the mandated schedule for all of the six days he earns a gold medal.

Ted was bent on his third gold. He had run four months of qualifying races, earned a spot on the American team, and been assigned a number and a departure time, or "key time," for the opening day of the race. He had his plane ticket, his cycle in a crate, and his gear in the duffles when he was critically injured in an automobile accident September 4. For two and a half weeks he lay in an intensive-care ward in a more or less comatose state. With hearts heavier than their cycles or their gear, Ted's brother and his comrades flew off to France without him.

At 2:45 a.m. on the first day of the Six Days' Teddy burst an artery in his chest; the doctor and nurses were at a loss to explain this serious and unexpected complication. But they didn't know our Ted, his total concentration on his singular passion. Ted was to have been off the line at 8:08 that morning. When he exerted the strain that burst his damaged artery, it was 2:45 a.m. in Ohio but in the south of France it was 8:45. Coincidence, perhaps. But no one speaks with certainty about the workings of the subconscious mind.

On the morning that would have marked the first of his senior year as an ag student at O.S.U. Ted's artery hemorrhaged again, too much this time for the once-powerful body.

The nights turned cold and the leaves changed color. South of the line where the land slopes toward the river, Teddy's soybeans ripened in the late September afternoon. The motorcycle trails to the lower flats were strewn with early-fallen leaves. Somewhere in the south of France the medals were awarded. On that day our son vanished into the green-gold paradise that had nurtured him. Nobody who knew him doubts that Teddy got his "gold."

Index

About the Author

One of Ed Youngblood's earliest memories while growing up in Oklahoma is of a man who rode a green Indian Chief by his house almost every day. He says, "I was transfixed by the sight and sound of that motorcycle. I would stand and watch until it disappeared, and continue to stand and watch the horizon until I could no longer hear its exhaust note." Youngblood bought his first motorcycle at the age of 14, and has owned and ridden motorcycles for more than 40 years.

Following completion of a Bachelor of Arts degree at Oklahoma State University in 1965, and a Master of Arts degree in English Literature at Ohio University in 1968, he took a job as managing editor at *Cycle News East,* in Amherst, Ohio, the home town of John Penton. Coincidentally, the Penton motorcycle had been introduced just a few months before Youngblood and his wife, Margaret, arrived in Amherst.

In 1970 he was recruited by the American Motorcyclist Association to become managing editor of *American Motorcyclist* (at that time entitled *AMA News*), beginning a 28-year career with the Association. From head of the AMA's communications department he moved to direct its government relations program, then was appointed President and CEO in 1981, serving until mid-February, 1999.

During his service at the AMA, Youngblood helped establish the American Motorcycle Heritage Foundation, which opened the Motorcycle Hall of Fame Museum in 1990. He also served 25 years as an elected delegate to the Federation

Internationale de Motocycliste, based in Geneva, Switzerland. At the FIM he served more than 20 years as a vice president on its board of directors, rising to the position of Deputy President, the second-highest title in the organization. Upon his retirement from the FIM in 1996, he was named Honorary Deputy President, becoming one of only three individuals in the world to be granted that title.

Youngblood has served on boards and committees of various national organizations, including The Clayton Foundation, which raises and disburses funds to injured motorcycle racers, and the Motor Sports Hall of Fame in Novi, Michigan. In August 1998, he was inducted into The National Motorcycle Hall of Fame in Sturgis, South Dakota. In April 1999, he was named Man of the Year by the Women's Motocross League. In July 1999, he was inducted into The Motorcycle Hall of Fame at Pickerington, Ohio. In September 1999, he was presented the John Farmer Eggers Award, the highest honor bestowed by the Motorcycle Riders Foundation.

Although he has written hundreds of columns and articles for *American Motorcyclist* and other publications, *John Penton and the Off-Road Motorcycle Revolution* is his first book-length project. He and Margaret have two sons, Ruben and Christian.

The author, left, with John Penton and a 1998 KTM John Penton 30th
Anniversary limited edition. November 2, 1999.